T0286845

ANGELS
in Our Room

ANGELS
in Our Room

A Journey through the
Heartache of Infertility to the
Joy of Divine Purpose

GL Mendenhall

Forefront
BOOKS

Published by Forefront Books.
Distributed by Simon & Schuster.

Library of Congress Control Number: 2023910434

Print ISBN: 978-1-63763-216-1
E-book ISBN: 978-1-63763-217-8

Cover Design by Bruce Gore, Gore Studio, Inc.
Interior Design by Bill Kersey, KerseyGraphics

DEDICATION

McKenzie Brooke, our sweet girl,
Mom and Dad love you more than
words could ever express.

You are the answer to so many prayers.

We thank God daily for that
incredible early morning
He brought you to us, straight from heaven,
accompanied by angels in our room.

What an amazing journey you
have been on thus far.

Every time I sat down to write this
book, you were on my mind.

It has been my joy to write
an account of our lives,
knowing you will always have a reminder
of the many ways God has interceded for us.

As you continue to grow and navigate this life,
remember the same Creator God
Who handcrafted you
from the beginning, will never leave you.

He will be your guide when you need
direction, your joy in times of sorrow,
and your help in times of need.

I am blessed beyond measure to be your mom.

I love you forever and always.

This book is for you.

CONTENTS

PREFACE

IN 1999 MY HUSBAND JASON STARTED HIS twenty-year military career as a naval aviator and flight instructor. We experienced many ups and downs, but more joy than sorrow, as we navigated through numerous moves across the country. After 9/11, he was deployed to Iraq, Afghanistan, and many other overseas locations.

It was during our time in California, while he was training for his first deployment, that we started talking about having a baby. We had been married for close to four years and were newly stationed at Lemoore Naval Air Station. I can still remember the day I called family and friends from our little apartment, telling them with excitement how Jason and I had decided to start trying to have a family. I smiled with anticipation as I looked through my hope chest—a chest of baby clothes I had started to collect when I was just a teenager, in hopes of one day having a child of my own. I could not believe the time had come to use those clothes and baby items I had collected through the years. I was beyond excited as I dreamed of what it would be like to experience pregnancy, pick out a name, decorate a nursery, and feel the joy of raising a child. We had so much to look forward to. We were so ready!

Never could we have imagined we would face nearly ten years of infertility. There would be a myriad of doctor's appointments, medical procedures, fertility medicine, and even exploratory surgery that would diagnosis me with multiple issues preventing pregnancy. I remember the day my doctor told me the results of his exploratory surgery. His heart was broken as he shared the disappointing news: polycystic ovarian syndrome, fibroid tumors, endometriosis...all tough stuff. Just one of these diagnoses could prevent pregnancy, but I had multiple diagnoses to deal with. He told me then this would be an uphill battle and the chance of me conceiving on my own was extremely low. I was devastated. I went home after my appointment and cried for hours. Jason held me as he held back tears of his own.

However, we were not without hope! We held on to our faith in a God who had proven faithful to us time and time again throughout our lives. We knew He would continue to guide us every step of the way, because that's what our God does! He guides His children. He delights in His children. He wants good things for us even more than we want them for ourselves. We knew He would not fail us. The waiting was tough, but we believed if we were meant to have a child, it would be in God's time, and oh, what an experience it was when His timing came about!

This book is our miracle story, so you probably already know the outcome. God blessed us with a beautiful baby girl in 2013. She is our miracle, for sure! However, this miracle story is not just about our infertility journey and how we finally conceived. The miracle is *how* we found out we were pregnant. It was an experience literally sent from heaven above to confirm our pregnancy nine days before it was medically possible to be detected. We have shared this story with churches, family, friends, and even strangers. Every time we share it, people's hearts are moved and touched in such a special way, not because of anything we have said or done, but because the story is truly a miracle with no other explanation than it was orchestrated by God, revealing how every life comes about only when it is ordained by Him. There are no accidents.

Every life that exists is specifically crafted by Him. God let Jason and I have a literal glimpse of the psalmist's description:

For You created my inmost being;
You knit me together in my mother's womb.
I praise You because I am fearfully
and wonderfully made;
your works are wonderful,
I know that full well.
My frame was not hidden from You
when I was made in the secret place,
when I was woven together in
the depths of the earth.
Your eyes saw my unformed body;
all the days ordained for me were
written in your book
before one of them came to
be. (PSALM 139:13–16, NIV)

Chapter 1

IN THE BEGINNING

ASON AND I HEARD ABOUT EACH OTHER through family and friends months before we actually met. We were both born in 1976 and had similar backgrounds, as we were both raised in small Midwest towns. He was from Indiana, a Hoosier basketball fan through and through. I was from a small farming town in Illinois. Eventually, life brought us both to the East Coast, which is where our story together begins.

Numerous people inside both our circles seemed to think we would be a good match, including my mother and brother, who had each separately met Jason before I did. They could not have been more right! In the fall of 1997, Jason and I met, and after spending time together at various church events and outings with mutual friends, we planned our first date for January. By then, Jason was in his junior year at the United States Naval Academy in Annapolis, Maryland, and I was a music teacher at a private school nearby. Neither one of us were looking for anything serious, but from that first date, we knew we had something special.

We went out for the first time to Silver Diner, a nostalgic restaurant that had quickly become one of my favorites after having moved to the area just a few short years before. I loved that little diner with its charming 1950s décor. The jukebox was playing in the background as we placed our order for cheeseburgers, fries, and milkshakes in that quaint, old-fashioned, red corner booth.

We quickly picked up on each other's sense of humor that night, and we played off each other as we managed to convince our waitress we were there to celebrate our one-year wedding anniversary. We all had a good laugh after we let her in on the joke, but she almost didn't believe us. She had watched our interaction all night and couldn't believe we were not an actual couple.

"No way this is y'all's first date!" the waitress exclaimed.

She saw the same chemistry between us others had seen, and we were beginning to feel it too.

We also found out we had a lot in common; we shared a love for music, travel, movies, and yes, engaging in the occasional practical joke. It really was a perfect first date getting to know each other better, asking a million questions about this and that, and making plans to see each other again.

The next day, I found out Jason was quite the romantic. He sent me a beautiful bouquet of red roses with the most charming handwritten note, which read, "I think I forgot something in your car last night...my heart."

That card made me smile for days. Not long after, we started dating exclusively and he continued to send the sweetest daily correspondence to me, mostly through the relatively new technology of email. Remember the movie *You've Got Mail*? I couldn't wait to hear those words! At the beginning of our relationship, we lived nearly an hour apart, so we saw each other mostly on weekends. These were the days of landline telephones with expensive long-distance calls, and since neither one of us had large bank accounts, email became one of

❧

We had a lot in common;
we shared a love for
music, travel, movies,
and yes, engaging in the
occasional practical joke.

❧

the most effective ways to get to know each other over the first few months of dating. He would write daily to say hello and see how my day went. There was usually some kind of hilarious poem included, followed by compliments galore, always genuine and heartfelt.

A month after our first date, on Valentine's Day, he surprised me by renting a plane and flying me over the Potomac River; yep, he was a pilot. He played my favorite songs through my headset as we flew around in that little four-seat Cessna. Although this was such a romantic gesture and I was thoroughly impressed, I secretly could not wait to get back on the ground. He didn't realize I was a bit of a nervous flier; we hadn't yet discussed it. I was especially nervous in small planes. Add flying over a body of water, and I could no longer hide my concern. Noticing my relief upon landing, he asked if I was okay. I explained to him that, although it was the sweetest, most romantic surprise, flying in a tiny plane over water while listening to the *Titanic* theme song "My Heart Will Go On" and envisioning Jack and Rose freezing in the water below, made me very glad my feet were planted back on the ground! We laughed throughout the rest of the evening as we recalled that adventurous little plane ride.

We were having a great time together as we continued to date. It seemed there was always some special event to get dressed up for, like the Naval Academy's Ring Dance or dinner in Washington, DC, for a navy celebration. Whatever the occasion, he always looked handsome dressed in his Whites or Navy Blues. When he would escort me to an event, he seemed so proud to have me on his arm, treating me as if I were the most important person there.

As I continued to get to know him, I grew to admire many things about his character. His love and respect for his parents, the elderly, and his country was evident. He's funny as all get out, and to my delight, is musically talented. I still love hearing him play the saxophone.

To no one's surprise, we fell for each other quickly. My family and friends loved him right away; likewise his parents with me. It was an extraordinarily happy time in our lives, and I haven't even mentioned the marriage proposal yet!

It was June 1998 and Bill Clinton was president. Jason was taking a few extra classes at Georgetown as part of the summer studies program at Annapolis, which included working in Washington as an intern. Jason asked me, very last minute, to attend a dinner party with him put on by the internship committee at a restaurant in DC atop Hotel Washington. It was nice he had asked me, of course, but I politely declined when I found out the dinner would be held in the early evening of the last day of school where I was working as a music teacher. Any teacher reading this book will relate to how exhausting the last day of school can be. I felt I wouldn't have near enough time to go home, change, and get myself presentable for such a dressy event since I'd have to leave for dinner almost as soon as my workday ended.

I felt terrible to decline since it seemed he really wanted to attend this dinner, so I suggested he take our friend Dan instead of me. Looking back, this was hilarious…because Jason's plan was to propose that night. I kept insisting he try to find someone else to go with him! Jason somehow sweet-talked me into it. Reluctantly, and cluelessly, I agreed to go.

A driver from the internship committee was going to meet me at my house after work and drive me to the restaurant, where he and the rest of the interns would be waiting.

I finished my hectic last day of school, rushed home, and found the driver already parked and waiting for me in the driveway. I hate for anyone to be waiting on me, but at this point, with glitter from homemade goodbye cards all over my shirt and my hair a mess, I had no choice but to go in, clean up, and get ready to head out for dinner as quickly as I could. I managed to change and freshen up in about fifteen minutes—quite a feat for me. I felt a bit disheveled, but I was happy I made it into a dress and had a chance to put my hair up. My good ol' Aqua Net did the trick to keep my hair up and high to the heavens!

I hurriedly hopped into the car, prepared to enjoy the hour ride and conversation with who I thought to be a worker from the internship committee. Unknown to me, Jason had personally rented the black Lincoln Town Car and driver, who played his part to a tee! I asked him all sorts of questions about his job at the committee and how long he and Jason had worked together. He didn't miss a beat as he told me how much he enjoyed working with Jason and how much he thought I would enjoy this dinner we were headed to.

Sometime during the ride, I received a call from Jason on my cellphone. I could hear a little stress in his voice as he apologized and let me know we would not be able to attend the dinner after all. He explained to me and the driver that his boss from the committee had called and informed him that, instead of dinner, they would now need him to pick up a package for Senator John McCain at, of all places, the White House! The new plan was for us to go pick Jason up and head out right away to get the package. What a whirlwind! I had made such an effort to get home and get ready so we'd make the dinner on time only to find out we were now heading to the White House! *What in the world? I thought.*

We picked up Jason, and not long after, we arrived at the East Gate of the White House. I remember the extraordinary security: the surveillance cameras, road barricades, uniformed guards, and Secret Service agents intensely keeping watch. Jason got out of the car and, much to my surprise, came and opened my door.

"Okay, we're here," he said. "Let's go!"

"What do you mean?" I questioned. "*You* work for these people, not me! Look at all these Secret Service agents around here. No way they're going to let me in. I'm staying right here in this car."

Jason later explained how, at that moment, he really was a bit worried. *Great,* he thought. *I've worked for weeks and weeks on this proposal, made it past the dinner cover story, got her to the White House, and now I'm not gonna be able to get her out of the car to go in with me!*

The driver, seeing my concern and desire to stay in the car, again didn't miss a beat. He reassured me he picked up packages from the White House all the time and they would certainly let me in if I was with Jason. He no doubt helped to save Jason's day! I still wasn't as convinced as the driver, but I reluctantly agreed to at least try to get in with Jason.

Of course, none of this would have ever happened under normal circumstances. As I would later learn, Jason had been working for well over a month to see whether a marriage proposal would be approved by the White House. He had to complete all the necessary background check paperwork required for me to gain access. By the time I ended up at the White House, I was so disorientated from everything happening so quickly, I didn't have much time to think about how unrealistic it would be for the Secret Service to let me into the White House with just a driver's license and Jason's word that I was not a threat to national security. It was all quite comical!

As we walked from the parking lot to the White House, everyone we encountered was in on the plan. We walked up to the gate, where Jason told the guard we were there to pick up a package for Senator McCain. The guard asked Jason for his ID and pretended to find

Jason's name listed on a roster granting him entrance. He then looked at me and in a very grumpy tone asked, "And who exactly are you? I don't see your name listed. Do you work for the committee as well?"

"No," I said. "I'm... with him. Here's my ID."

I was so nervous as I watched the guard's expressions of aggravation. He was obviously perturbed we were trying to get me into the White House without being on that list! I also noticed a plainclothes Secret Service agent in the distance watching all this go down and I just wanted to run back to the car! They all played their parts very well.

The guard looked at me, again very perturbed, and said, "Well, I really shouldn't let you in. You should be on this list. I guess I'll trust this guy and take his word you are who you say you are. Here's your ID back. You both may proceed."

At that moment, I didn't know whether I should enjoy the relief I felt or just kick Jason in the butt for getting me into this mess! I didn't even want to go to dinner in the first place. Now I wasn't even at the dinner; I was getting scolded by a guard for trying to get into the White House without proper clearance! I looked at Jason and told him he was so fired.

"Fired by who?" he questioned.

"Me!" I exclaimed.

Jason gave me a wink and said, "Well, we're getting in now so just enjoy it."

We were led into the East Wing reception hall where we signed the guest book and waited for President Clinton's naval aide, who was the son-in-law of the Naval Academy's superintendent, Chuck Larson. Jason had reached out to him as the central contact to help make all this happen for us. When the naval aide arrived, he shook our hands and introduced himself as though it was the first time he and Jason had ever talked. He thanked us for coming to get the package for the senator. He informed us the package was in another part of the White House, and to my delight he asked us if we would like a tour since we were already there.

A private tour of the White House from the president's naval aide? Yes, please! It was all happening so fast I didn't have time to comprehend that these kinds of things don't just happen without planning. Again, I was completely oblivious. Everyone played their part so well, it was seamless.

He led us through the halls of the White House where we saw original commissioned paintings of the presidents, the Green Room, and the China Room.

Dishes are my thing, so I was thrilled to see all the china patterns displayed from the former first ladies. We made our way briefly to the West Wing where we were able to look into the Oval Office and walk by the Rose Garden. It was truly amazing. By this time, I was extremely glad Jason had talked me into coming on this excursion, but I still had no idea it was about to become even better!

We were led into the First Lady's Garden and told to wait there for someone from the office to bring us Senator McCain's package. We enjoyed the landscape as we waited. I was still trying to comprehend how I ended up in the First Lady's Garden when just an hour before I was in a car headed to dinner. I was extremely excited, but I was careful to act prim and proper, acutely aware of the extraordinary security and Secret Service agents all around, particularly those just a few yards away on the South Lawn, where the president was hosting a reception for a foreign head of state. I couldn't help but feel nervous, especially since, as far as I knew, I wasn't even supposed to be there in the first place.

A few minutes later, a nice gentleman from the office walked up to us with a medium-sized manila envelope labeled "For Senator McCain." He handed it to Jason and asked us to remain in the garden until the naval aide returned to escort us out of the White House. Jason and I, still quietly being watched by Secret Service agents in the background, were standing together chatting, when Jason unexpectedly looked down at the package and said, "I wonder what's in here? It doesn't look taped up. Think I should open it and take a quick peek?"

I about came unglued!

"Are you kidding me?"

I whispered those words out of the side of my mouth and managed to look expressionless, but I'm pretty sure Jason deciphered it correctly as the "I'm-gonna-kill-you stink-eye look of death" I intended it to be.

"Look at the cameras and the guards! Don't you dare open that package," I said quietly but firmly.

You know exactly what Jason did! Yep! He started to open that package. I literally thought, *I must be standing next to an absolute idiot! I mean, he's attending a service academy, I thought he was supposed to be smart. He obviously is not!*

I was mortified. He showed no signs of stopping. He appeared determined to open that package. All I could do at that point was turn and start to walk away.

I didn't want to be any part of it. As I was walking away, I heard Jason holler, "Babe, wait!"

I turned around to find him down on one knee, with the opened package on his lap, holding a ring in his hand.

I can't begin to describe the flood of emotions I felt in that moment! The realization that it was all a setup. The dinner invitation being a cover for the most elaborate wedding proposal I could have imagined. My former thought of his idiocy just seconds before quickly changed. He was no longer an idiot; he was brilliant! My exhaustion from a hard day at work, my confusion about canceled dinner plans, my excitement and nervousness about trying to get into the White House, the thrill of the tour, the mortification of him opening a US senator's package, and the absolute exhilaration of seeing him down on one knee was almost too much! I broke down and cried. I tried to catch my breath as I listened to the sweetest words.

"Babe," he said with tears in his eyes. "I love you. I can't imagine my life without you in it. I'd like to ask my first lady, in our nation's First Lady's Garden, if you'll be my wife. Will you marry me?"

"Of course! Yes, YES!" I exclaimed.

~

"Babe," he said with tears in his eyes. "I love you. I can't imagine my life without you in it. I'd like to ask my first lady, in our nation's First Lady's Garden, if you'll be my wife. Will you marry me?"

"Of course! Yes, YES!" I exclaimed.

~

We cried and hugged as the guards and Secret Service agents nearby clapped and hollered out their congratulations. In one single moment, those slightly scary and formidable-looking guards now seemed so very sweet as they smiled and expressed their excitement for us. President Clinton's naval aide, who had been watching from a distance, walked back out to meet us, smiling from ear to ear. We will be forever grateful to him and the entire White House staff for helping make this incredible event happen.

After we left the White House, Jason had dinner set up for us at Hotel Washington after all, so we dined, taking in the beautiful American monuments nearby, laughing, crying, and recounting one of the most amazing days ever! People used to say we were living a fairy tale and, in some ways, it felt like it to us as well. It was an incredible time in our lives as we celebrated our engagement and planned our future together!

Chapter 2

IN GOOD TIMES
AND BAD

W E WERE MARRIED ON A BEAUTIFUL AFTERNOON in May 1999, three days after Jason graduated. We were so in love and didn't particularly care for the service academies' rule against students marrying before graduation. We would have likely married sooner if we could have, but we settled for three days after graduation. Adding a wedding at the end of the Academy's graduation sure made for a busy week, but oh, how exciting a week it was!

Jason looked so handsome wearing his traditional Service Dress White uniform and I loved my wedding dress, puffed sleeves and all! My dress had an antique vibe with a long ruffled train that I adored. It was extra special to me because it belonged to my cousin, who wore it on her wedding day almost ten years earlier. Our wedding colors were navy blue and gold for obvious reasons. My mom is a very talented floral arranger, and she did a beautiful job with all the decorations. She made my bouquet and decorated the entire venue, which will always be so special to me.

Our wedding party was large, made up of family and dear friends. My beautiful sister was my matron of honor, and both her and my brother sang a song with me during the ceremony as we welcomed Jason into our family. We were honored to have Jason's dad marry us and my brother-in-law direct the videotaping of the ceremony.

It was such a special wedding—filled with so many people we loved. We couldn't have asked for a better day. Everything went as planned except for our limo, which never showed. That, however, turned out to be one of the best parts of the day; Jason's two best men and groomsmen quickly swarmed his little blue Saturn sports coupe, decorating it the old-fashioned way, complete with toilet paper wrapping and stringed cans on the tailpipe. You should have seen me trying to get in that tiny car with my huge dress!

We drove around downtown Washington, my head sticking out of the sunroof waving at every car we passed, and Jason honking at pedestrians who waved to us from the busy sidewalks. As we drove around our nation's capital, we recalled our engagement story as we drove past the White House. We were thankful the limo never showed as we excitedly made our way around town, just taking it all in.

What an incredible week it was, followed by a relaxing honeymoon in a quaint cabin in the Great Smoky Mountains of Tennessee. When we arrived back, we moved into our first apartment eager to start the next chapter of our lives together.

Jason's first assignment after graduation was several months working in the Pentagon's Office of Legislative Affairs. He would get up early and ride the Metro to and from work, reading his beloved sports section of the *Washington Times*. This was a fun time for both of us—newly married, enjoying life in Washington. Many of our weekends were filled exploring all the city had to offer. We toured the national museums, monuments, and area battlefields. We loved riding the many bike paths throughout the city as well. We enjoyed plays, concerts, and a wide array of diverse cuisine not easily found in our small hometowns. We look back at our time in DC and Annapolis with great nostalgia, and we still love to visit. They are two amazing cities that, in many ways, played a huge part in shaping who we would become. Our experience in the area contributed to our love for and pride of this great nation, and it afforded us the opportunity to make lasting friendships that continue to be cherished to this day.

Several months later, it was time to move on, not only from Jason's job at the Pentagon but to another city entirely, where he would pursue his childhood dream of an aviation career. He knew since he was in third grade he wanted to fly. Like many kids growing up, his bedroom walls were covered with posters of his favorite jets and his room filled with aviation books and model airplanes. He knew his grades would be important, so he made studying a priority even at a young age because this would help him obtain scholarships and even one day, perhaps, get accepted into a military academy. He flew his first solo flight in an airplane on his sixteenth birthday and received his private pilot's license on his seventeenth birthday. With the help of his teachers, guidance counselors, parents, and many friends along the way, Jason was accepted into all three service academies, but his heart remained focused on naval aviation.

He was absolutely thrilled when, in his senior year at the Naval Academy, he and his roommates received their final service assignments to join the flight program! We would be based near his parents in Oklahoma for a short time, where the navy and air force were conducting a new joint pilot training program.

The very fact Jason was accepted into the navy's flight program was a miracle of God in itself. Although his academics, extracurriculars, and medical status were right where they needed to be, the navy has strict regulations requiring pilots to have twenty-twenty vision. At the time, pilots were not allowed to have a corrected prescription with glasses or laser eye surgery, and Jason had been wearing glasses on and off since the eighth grade. The long hours of studying—a necessity if you wanted to graduate from the Academy—hadn't improved his eyesight either, and he knew this could be a problem as he neared graduation. Like he often does, though, he kept his head down, diligently working, knowing that if it was meant to be, God would make a way.

Jason and I were raised to believe in the power of prayer. Not to sound cliché, but we truly believe God can make a way when there seems to be no other way. Jason's parents, godparents, and home church congregation gathered around him during one of his leave periods as final eye testing for the flight program neared. They anointed him with oil, as was done in biblical times, and prayed in faith, believing God would heal his eyes and allow him to pursue his desire to become a naval aviator. God honored their faith and it was done! Jason has passed every eye exam since that day with uncorrected twenty-twenty vision! This same power of God has protected Jason, opened doors and opportunities, and made a way for us throughout his military and civilian careers too many times to count. Every time we have been in need, God has provided. Every time we've asked for direction, He has guided us.

In this case, Jason's faith literally became sight as we moved to Oklahoma for him to start flight school! Although we lived in Oklahoma for only about six months, it was an intense six months. Jason and his fellow student pilots navigated through long days and nights of tough curriculum and flight training. This was the first glimpse for me into what life as a military spouse sometimes looks like. It was a big adjustment as

❧

Every time we have been
in need, God has provided.
Every time we've asked for
direction, He has guided us.

❧

we didn't have quite as much time to spend with each other during the week as we once had. Jason would be at the military base for twelve hours at a time and come home with barely enough time for dinner; then he would go right back to studying for his next flight. It was challenging for both of us, but we kept putting one foot in front of the other while doing our best to encourage each other that the effort would be worth it. By the time the weekend came, he was understandably exhausted, so we would take the weekend to rest and spend some much-needed time together. Jason's dad pastored a church nearby, after having retired from Boeing in Wichita, so we looked forward to seeing him and Jason's mother as well. His dad's sermons and his mom's home cooking always did us good!

Our six months in Oklahoma came to an end, and we moved to Mississippi, where Jason continued his flight training at Naval Air Station Meridian. I loved living in Mississippi, with its gorgeous landscapes, abundant hardwood forests, and many rivers. It's such a beautiful state, and the city of Meridian is no exception. It is a lovely area, smelling of magnolia blooms in the spring and pine trees in the fall. Charming historic homes and businesses of many architectural styles are evident throughout the Queen City, as Meridian is affectionately called. We were excited to experience the city's music and art scene and enjoy some homestyle southern cuisine. We found a cute little town house to rent, and I started unpacking as Jason got settled into his new squadron. I found a part-time job as an office manager for a bed and breakfast reservation service. Many of the bed and breakfasts we reserved were for historic antebellum mansions throughout the state of Mississippi. Considering how much I love the South, this was an extraordinarily fun job for me. On occasion, Jason and I would travel around the state to visit and enjoy these historic properties.

Two months after our move to Mississippi, we celebrated our one-year wedding anniversary. Jason outdid himself once again, going out of his way to make this a special occasion for me. The morning of our anniversary he told me we would celebrate by going out to dinner that night. He left for the base that morning, or so I thought, right before I left for work. I came home early afternoon to find a note on our front door—a poem actually. That note was a clue to go find the location of the next note. I found the next poem on the fireplace mantel under a favorite candle. The next note led me outside to the mailbox. The poem inside the mailbox led me to the gas station down the road, where the gas station attendant handed me the next note with a rose. That note led me back home, where Jason had snuck back inside while I was at the gas station. When I opened the door to the house this time, there were rose petals leading me upstairs. I opened the door to our bedroom to find a beautiful, large wall mirror from Pier 1 Imports that I had been wanting, with a bow hanging from it. On the mirror was the final note:

I wish you could see yourself through my eyes. Then you'd truly know the depth of my love for you. When you look into this mirror, let it be a reminder of how beautiful you are inside and out. Happy anniversary, babe!

Jason then poked his head out of our bathroom where he was hiding, handed me a bouquet of roses, and gave me a big hug and kiss. This was my guy—a romantic-scavenger-hunt kind of guy. Always thoughtful; ornery at times, but such a sweetie.

Around one year later he completed flight school with distinction and received his navy wings! His parents, god-parents, and two of his best buddies attended the winging ceremony, in which I and Jason's dad had the honor of pinning on his "wings of gold."

We became very fond of life in Mississippi, especially the fishing, hunting, crawfish boils, and trips to the coast. So when Jason was offered the opportunity to stay in Mississippi as a flight instructor before taking his first fleet assignment, we jumped at it. Jason would now be a SERGRAD (Selectively Retained Graduate) for about a year and a half, flying with and training new students, many of whom were his classmates from Annapolis. He loved it. As for me…well, it's a dangerous occupation, and this newly married wife had her concerns. However, I was always reminded that God had specifically made a way for him to be in this very occupation, so I trusted He would protect him.

Our time in Mississippi came to an end after almost three years. We met wonderful people there, not only at the Naval Air Station but also at a little Nazarene church in Meridian. The pastors and staff guided and encouraged us, and many of the church members are some of our best friends to this day. As we left for California in January 2003, we had no idea that we would come back to live in Mississippi or that it would be the backdrop for the most life-changing event we'd ever experience!

Moving to California was an adventure. Jason was picked to join Navy Strike Fighter Squadron VFA-122 in Lemoore, where he would train to fly the F/A-18E Super Hornet and ultimately join VFA-115 for his first combat deployment to Iraq. I was so proud of him.

There was certainly a lot happening with Jason's schedule. He was in and out of town for multiple training exercises, so I was on my own a good bit. I kept busy unpacking our little apartment on base. I love to decorate; it's a huge hobby of mine, so I took my time decorating and getting settled into our new place as well as familiarizing myself with the town of Lemoore.

I enjoyed being a military spouse, but it brings with it a multitude of challenges. As many know, the enormous amount of time away from loved ones can be tough, to say the least. Learning to navigate new states, cities, and neighborhoods, many times on our own, can be challenging. Finding jobs as a military spouse can prove difficult as well.

Résumé gaps from frequent moves are common and sometimes hard to overcome. I eventually started a part-time job as a physical therapist aide, although my love of music continued to be my priority. As in Mississippi, there were no teaching positions in the field of music available at the time of my move to California, but I still made time to travel and sing for several events throughout the country. I was also involved in our squadron spouse club, which was a great support system for me and many other spouses facing similar challenges.

The biggest change for me, personally, was in our pursuit to start a family. After four years of marriage, we were so ready for children. I still remember the day I called family and friends from our little base apartment and told them Jason and I were going to start trying to have a baby. They were all so excited, particularly Jason's parents. The thought of another added family member thrilled them, especially since Jason was an only child. I saw my doctor several times throughout my time in California as I noticed my monthly cycles were irregular, accompanied by a great deal of pain. I knew this could potentially cause difficulty getting pregnant, but I was young and wasn't too worried about it at that point, so we continued to talk about and plan for a family with excitement.

About a year later, right before Jason left for his first six-month deployment, we decided to buy our first house. Our apartment on base was quite small, so we were happy to be moving into a home with four bedrooms. When family and friends came to visit us from out of town, I would lead them past the office to the guest room and let them know that the room across the hallway would hopefully very soon be used as a nursery.

I showed them the baby books I bought and had read a dozen times. I showed them my very long list of baby names I had started to write down. Some said I looked like I was glowing just talking about it. I agreed with them! Just the thought of being a mother thrilled me. Looking back I recognize that, even as a teenager, I was preparing for motherhood. I was always collecting baby items at garage sales or consignment stores. Back then, hope chests were popular. I'd see little ruffled dresses, pajamas, or bibs and couldn't resist buying them. Into my hope chest they'd go! All in preparation for a precious baby.

In our new house, at twenty-seven years old, I longed to be a mother. I ached for it. And Jason was equally excited. He listened attentively as I shared with him all I had learned from my pregnancy books. He teared up when I showed him pictures of a baby's development in the womb from the incredible book *A Child is Born*. We discussed names, nursery colors, and future trips to Disney World with our little one. Anything and everything about a future child was on our minds.

We both kept busy with life, however. Over the course of the next four years, Jason would be deployed multiple times throughout the world. On occasion, I was able to travel to see him during port calls. One memorable port call was in Dubai, UAE. What a trip! The best part, of course, was getting to see Jason after months of separation. However, I really did experience a whole new world. The culture, landscape, food, and interaction with this country's people were unlike anything I'd ever experienced in my many travels. I shopped at the outdoor spice markets and was captivated by the beauty I saw. The aroma from baskets of spices in every color of the rainbow filled the whole market area. I bought frankincense and myrrh, which I thought was the coolest thing. We went on a desert safari, which included a camel ride and an outrageously exciting Jeep excursion through the sand dunes. When the sun set, we sat under handmade tents and ate authentic Emirati food under the stars in the middle of the desert. What amazing memories!

In between deployments, we still had a full schedule. Jason would resume training on the base, I was working and learning the ropes of a PT aide, and we would travel on the weekends, exploring the beautiful state of California. Carmel-by-the-Sea is, to this day, one of my favorite places ever. Many of this quaint city's homes and businesses look like they came right out of a magical storybook. We drove the coastline of Highway 1, visited Big Sur, hiked the trails of Yosemite, and reveled at the site of the magnificent sequoias as well as Kings Canyon. Some of the most beautiful landscapes and national parks on the planet are in California, and we took advantage of visiting them every chance we got. Even though we were busy with work and exploring the state, the desire to start a family was always present and never far from our thoughts. We would see families at squadron parties playing and laughing with their little ones and would smile at each other, knowing each other's thoughts— that we couldn't wait for our turn to come.

However, our attempts at pregnancy in California were not successful. We never used that set-aside room in our house as a nursery. Countless pregnancy tests came back negative as we tried month after month. My childhood friends were getting pregnant; some already had several children. Ladies in the squadron were busy with their families, some having just given birth. As much as I truly was happy for them, it seemed to highlight the fact that I still was not pregnant. I was truly sad, and age was starting to be more of a concern for me. By the end of our time in California, I had just turned thirty, and I surmised I had some classic textbook reasons why pregnancy was not happening for me.

First, as mentioned already, was my age. Women thirty and older can start to have issues simply because they are getting older. Ovulation can become harder or nonexistent, depending on the health of their ovaries. Women thirty-five and older can start to have more dangerous complications as well. Not only can it be harder to conceive after the age of thirty-five, but it also comes with an increased risk for miscarriage. All these statistics were on my mind and caused me a great deal of anxiety.[*]

Second, several women in my family, including my mother and sister, had dealt with infertility issues. I had always known it could affect me as well, but I had no idea to what extreme.

Third, we were under a great deal of stress. Although our time in California was filled with good times and wonderful memories, the fact that Jason was training and preparing for deployment was always a concern for me, and it certainly kept him on his toes. Preparation for Jason and his fellow fighter pilots included practicing complicated tactical flight maneuvers and

[*] "Age and Fertility," Better Health Channel, Department of Health of the State Government of Victoria, accessed May 31, 2023, https://www.betterhealth.vic. gov.au/health/conditionsandtreatments/age-and-fertility.

proficiency landings on and off aircraft carriers at sea. His job was dangerous, whether he was at home training or deployed overseas. Both of us, along with our military friends and families, were feeling the life stressors that come along with being a part of an active deployable squadron.

Again, I suspected that all these reasons could have been possible contributing factors for my inability to get pregnant during our time in California. Although I understood it, I couldn't help but be disappointed that all these years had passed with no pregnancy success. However, we held on to our faith that it would happen in God's time, and we focused on the fact that Jason was home safe, having several deployments behind him.

As our time in California came to an end, we were so thankful to God for His protection over Jason and his shipmates, as well as for sustaining me and the other military spouses and families during the time away from our loved ones. After the exciting and fast-paced life of the fleet, we were both thrilled to find out his new assignment, as requested, was back in Meridian, Mississippi, where we looked forward to having a bit more downtime. Jason would once again be a flight instructor, passing his experiences along to the next

❧

We held on to our faith that it would happen in God's time.

❧

generation of fighter pilots. Although it was still a dangerous job, after several deployments during active combat, Mississippi was a welcomed duty station. So back to Mississippi we went!

Chapter 3

THE STRUGGLE IS REAL

IN JANUARY 2007, WE WERE BUSY GETTING BACK into our daily routines in Mississippi. Jason was preparing to start flight instruction again at Naval Air Station Meridian, and, after years of part-time jobs, I had decided to enroll at Mississippi State University to pursue a degree in psychology. We moved into a beautiful home (pictured on the cover) with almost eight acres of land. When our Realtor showed us the house, my first thought was how perfect this place would be to raise a family!

The home sat back off the road and up on a hill. It was surrounded by such a gorgeous landscape. Pine, oak, dogwood, Japanese maple, and magnolia trees ran throughout the property. Azaleas, lavender bushes, and even bamboo surrounded the house. There was a koi pond outside the kitchen window and a brick pathway starting at the front of the house that ran all the way down the hill, through the woods, until you reached a small wooden bridge that crossed a tiny stream. Quaint light posts followed the pathway down the hill to the entrance of the driveway. As you continued to the other side of the property, there were apple and pear trees and even a small area formerly used as a vineyard. It truly was our dream house.

We were thankful to God for blessing us with such a lovely place and couldn't wait to start a family there. I spent a good part of that year unpacking and settling in. I enjoyed painting and making cosmetic changes to the home's interior to make it feel like our own. While attending college full time kept me extremely busy, starting a family was never far from my heart and mind. Although we had tried to conceive throughout our time in California, I hadn't gone through any specific testing. After being unsuccessful for such a long time, I knew I had to make testing a priority.

In between house projects and school assignments that year, I saw my family doctor, who referred me to a well-respected ob-gyn in our community. I told him about our inability to get pregnant and asked what next steps he suggested. He had a very tender heart regarding our struggle. As a pilot also, he enjoyed flying whenever he could and had a special connection with Jason. Many of our appointments started with him requesting an update on what Jason was up to at the navy base.

Our doctor outlined a plan and ran several tests on both of us to gain insight into what might be preventing pregnancy. Jason's test results showed no fertility issues. After reviewing my symptoms and past medical records, he recommended exploratory laparoscopy, a surgery to take a closer look into my abdomen.

Jason took me to the hospital and waited until surgery was complete. While still in recovery, the doctor told Jason the surgery went well and we would have the results in a couple of days. What was to be a relatively quick outpatient procedure turned into an extended stay as I had a terrible time recovering from the anesthesia. I was so nauseous and couldn't stop vomiting. They admitted me into a private room where Jason and my sweet nurse took care of me for more than six hours as I threw up continuously. I would sleep a little, wake up, and then throw up again. Every time I woke up, Jason and my nurse would rush over to the bedside. One would hold the pan for me, and the other would hold my hair back out of my face.

They had gotten to know each other fairly well as my recovery stretched through the afternoon and into the evening. My stomach started to settle, and we began to talk about my release from the hospital. Jason looked at this nurse he had been with for the past six hours and said with a straight face, "Well, you should probably go ahead and call GL's husband and let him know it's almost time for her to be picked up."

"Oh!" the nurse said. Her look of shock and confusion was evident. "I'm sorry," she continued. "I just assumed *you* were the husband?"

"Oh no," Jason said calmly, "I'm just her lover."

You should have seen this poor lady's face! As sick and tired as I still felt, I hee-hawed! I lifted my weak head up and muttered, "He's lying! Don't believe him. He's my husband and he's a mess!"

We all couldn't stop laughing! The relief on her face was priceless, and after a very tough day, I was now smiling. My husband's prankster spirit uplifted me that day and on many others in our infertility struggle.

After recovering a few days at home, the doctor's office called and said they had the test results back. The doctor wanted me to come back to the office to talk with him about his findings. Jason couldn't come with me since he was scheduled to work during my appointment but gave me a kiss goodbye before he left that morning. "Keep your chin up. Don't worry 'bout nothin'," he said, repeating a phrase his dad always says. "We'll talk about the results when I get back from work."

After studying and finishing some housework, I headed off to my appointment that afternoon. I sat nervously waiting for the doctor. I knew something was wrong after years of pain and irregular menstrual cycles, but I had no idea to what extent. As our doctor came in, I could see the disappointment on his face.

I was diagnosed with polycystic ovarian syndrome, which are cysts on my ovaries; multiple fibroid tumors in my uterus; and a severe case of endometriosis throughout my abdomen. These were all contributing factors for my pain and anovulation. Chronic anovulation is a common cause of infertility. My doctor's opinion was that I had most likely never ovulated in my entire life. Clearly, if I had never ovulated and had multiple issues continuing to prevent ovulation,

❧

As a wife, I couldn't help but

feel, if even for a moment,

that I was the problem.

❧

this was a big problem. As a wife, I couldn't help but feel, if even for a moment, that I was the problem. My doctor explained that, given my multiple diagnoses and considering my age of thirty-one, the chances of ever conceiving on my own were extremely low. Even with fertility medicine it would be an uphill battle to achieve pregnancy, with no guarantees.

The results were devastating to me. As I walked out of the door of the doctor's office, tears started to roll down my face. I barely made it to my car before those tears turned into sobbing. I opened the door and fell into the seat of my car. I cried out to God as I grieved the news that I might never be able to conceive and carry a child. The whole drive home, thoughts of worthlessness began to run through my mind.

Jason's test results are fine, I thought. *I am the problem. He will blame me. Sure, he loves me, but in time he will resent me if I can't give him a child.* I knew they were all lies of the enemy, but they bounced through my mind all the way home. I could barely see to drive I was crying so hard.

I arrived home a few hours before Jason did. He walked into the house eager to hear the results. He saw my eyes were red, tears still falling. I couldn't find the words to tell him. How do you tell your husband it

❧

I cried out to God as I
grieved the news that I
might never be able to
conceive and carry a child.

❧

doesn't look good? That chances were extremely low we would ever conceive on our own. I was somehow able to get the words out.

"We can try fertility medicine," I said, "but it's still a real possibility that in my condition even fertility medicine won't work. We may never be able to conceive."

As I look back and reflect upon that moment, I realize Jason's response could have been life-or-death to my spirit. The emotional pain I felt personally was unlike any I had experienced before. The guilt I felt, thinking I might be the cause of such a great loss for Jason, was indescribable. I literally felt broken. My heart was broken; my spirit was broken; my body was broken. He could have responded in so many ways. He could have shown his disappointment. He could have brought up the fact that I was the one with all the medical issues. He could have complained about the extra money it was going to cost for doctor's visits and fertility medicine.

Instead, he took me in his arms and held me. He told me he loved me and that we were in this together. He reminded me we were not without hope. He told me one way or another we would be parents, whether through conceiving or by the wonderful world of adoption, which has been such a special part of our extended family's lives. He dispelled the lies of the enemy floating around in my head with the truth that he loved me and God was in control of our future, so we would continue to trust Him.

That is a moment I won't forget. I went from a place of helplessness to a place of hope in a very short amount of time, all because my husband responded to me with a 1 Corinthians kind of love—a selfless love that rose above his own hurt and attended to my needs as though they were his own. I'm reminded of this verse often, as it was shown to me through Jason's actions that day:

> Love is patient, love is kind. It does not envy, it does not boast, it is not proud. It does not dishonor others, it is not self-seeking, it is not easily angered, it keeps no record of wrongs. Love does not delight in evil but rejoices with the truth. It always protects, always trusts, always hopes, always perseveres. Love never fails.
> (1 CORINTHIANS 13:4–8, NIV)

Now that we had some answers to what was preventing pregnancy, we carried on with our doctor's plan. He prescribed a low dose of Clomid, a fertility medicine that can help to balance hormones and assist with ovulation. I read all I could on infertility and talked to women with similar infertility stories as ours. I looked up healthy eating habits, cut back on caffeine, and tried anything that would possibly assist me in achieving pregnancy. I called family and friends and asked them to start praying. By this time, our local church knew our struggles and we were on many prayer lists. The years just kept on rolling by, however, with no success.

Negative ovulation and pregnancy tests were a common occurrence every month. As many times as I took these tests, you'd think I would have gotten used to that negative result, but I never did. Each time I had to tell Jason it didn't work, it felt as though another piece of my heart was being chipped away. I wasn't sure how many more negative tests I could bear to look at. Jason was always so comforting when I'd tell him the sad news, but I know it had to take a toll on him as well. I longed for the day I could look him in the eye and say, "It worked! We're pregnant!"

Another year passed, and the fertility medicine still wasn't working. My pain from physical symptoms continued to get worse. In 2009, Jason drove me to the ER where I had to have a blood transfusion due to blood loss. At that point my doctor said, "I know how much you want a pregnancy, but under most circumstances when I see symptoms this severe, I recommend a hysterectomy." He wanted to give me every opportunity at pregnancy, however, so he let me know he had done all he could do for me as an ob-gyn and recommended me to a fertility specialist.

I was busy with school during this time as well, working full time on my psychology degree. I was tired and stressed on many levels. I fought bouts of depression from the physical exhaustion of it all. Nevertheless, I remained hopeful as we contemplated seeing a specialist. We continued to bathe every step of our infertility journey in prayer, asking God to direct us to the right doctor and to give us wisdom over which procedures or medicine we should try next. In 2010, we started seeing an amazing fertility doctor ninety miles away in Jackson, Mississippi.

There was some very exciting progress made that year. With some added medicine taken at specific times, I was finally able to ovulate for maybe the first time in my life! When I saw that positive ovulation test, I was elated. I enthusiastically called family and friends to tell them the news. Looking back, I find it quite comical. I remember calling a lady in my church who had been praying for us to get pregnant. She didn't answer the phone, so I left a message that said, "I ovulated!" If that wasn't bad enough, after I hung up I remembered she shared her phone with her husband. It was probably a little shocking as they checked their messages and heard my boisterous voice deliver a quite personal bit of information. But I couldn't help myself! It was progress and I couldn't wait to share it.

Now that I was ovulating, we tried the next step in our process. Over the course of that year, we attempted artificial insemination three times. All three attempts failed, which was beyond disappointing. I was now in my third year of college, writing papers and working on projects. I was living alone; Jason was working overseas for most of that year, so his safety was always a concern for me. I was driving ninety miles one way for doctor's appointments and procedures. I was so worn out and had to practice counting my blessings often in order to get through it.

Please don't get me wrong. I don't want to sound ungrateful. I had so many blessings that I thanked God for every day, and no doubt these blessings were the reason I got through those tough times. Three such blessings were my precious mom and in-laws. They took me to many of my appointments in Jackson when

Jason was out of the country. They drove all those miles back and forth with me so I didn't have to travel alone. They, along with my sister and many friends, were constantly encouraging me through the sometimes mundane appointment schedules I had to keep up with. In fact, my in-laws took me to at least one of those artificial insemination appointments. When asked by a friend what I'd been up to that day, it was hilarious to reply, "Well, nothing much. My in-laws took me to get artificially inseminated, but other than that, nothing new going on!"

We always tried to keep things light, and of course, funny. Laughter can be the best medicine, and it is what helped me through so many tough times. Proverbs 17:22 says, "A joyful heart is good medicine, but a crushed spirit dries up the bones" (ESV).

I tried to practice having a joyful heart during so much of this disappointment. Many times, I was successful. Other times joy felt far away. My spirit was sometimes crushed. I never gave up believing that God heard our prayers, but waiting so long for His answer wasn't easy. I questioned the wait. I questioned the struggle. I had served God my whole life. As a kid, I sang at churches, revivals, and camp meetings, often missing out on ball games and after-school activities.

This entire time, I felt
God's grace covering me
during my questioning. I
never felt condemnation.
Not only did He not mind
my questions; He also gave
me the strength I needed
to wait for the answers.

My adult life was about ministry as well. I taught Sunday school, led worship, and often visited nursing homes to pray with and sing to the residents. Jason's life was about serving his country and serving others. We loved our family members and helped our church family when in need. Why couldn't we have a family of our own to love and take care of? Why wasn't God giving us the desires of our hearts like His Word promises us? Why was this process so hard for us, when it seemed so easy for so many others? Why was it taking so long? I had so many questions but no answers.

This entire time, I felt God's grace covering me during my questioning. I never felt condemnation. Not only did He not mind my questions; He also gave me the strength I needed to wait for the answers. Sometimes that strength came from His sweet Holy Spirit speaking to me through the words of a song or a Scripture verse. Sometimes it was through the prayers my momma and countless other family and friends prayed over me. Sometimes it was through a wink and a hug from Jason when he saw I was struggling. One of my favorite songs, written by Steven Curtis Chapman and Jerry Salley, says it so well: "His Strength Is Perfect"!

During our infertility journey, we looked into adoption on several occasions. We have a heart for adoption and were very open to it. At one point we looked into adopting two little girls, sisters in the foster care system. We were given pictures of them by their extended family and we prayed over these sweet girls daily. We were so excited at the possibility of raising them as our own. My heart was already invested in them as we waited on word of their placement. However, God had other plans for them. Another piece of my heart broke at yet another loss. We still felt that maybe adoption was the direction we were to pursue since our attempts at conceiving continued to fail. It was just so expensive—literally cost-prohibitive for us at the time.

We knew we would need a miracle either way. We needed a miracle to conceive or a miracle to afford adoption. Both options were unattainable on our own, but that's where God stepped in! When I look back at all the ways God showed Himself strong during this process, I can honestly say I would not change the struggle. Jason and I both believe that during the wait God taught us some of our most valuable lessons. When we were disappointed, we felt God's comfort. In our confusion, we felt His peace. And when we did not know which step to take next, we felt His guiding hand along the way. Sometimes there is purpose in the wait.

≈

They that wait upon the Lord shall renew their strength; they shall mount up with wings as eagles; they shall run, and not be weary; and they shall walk, and not faint. (ISAIAH 40:31, KJV)

Chapter 4

A FORK IN THE ROAD

IT HAD BEEN QUITE A YEAR. MY ER SCARE resulting in a blood transfusion and three failed artificial insemination procedures continued to take a toll on me. Although my age, now thirty-four, was a concern, I had to take a break from our fertility treatments. I was very close to finishing my degree in psychology and decided to postpone any more treatments as I tried to concentrate on finishing my last semester of college and prepare for graduation.

We also took a much-needed vacation. I had always wanted to visit Italy, and this beautiful country's culture and landscape did wonders for my psyche. We toured the Vatican in Rome, viewed Michelangelo's *David* in Florence, and took a gondola through the canals of Venice. We visited the Tower of Pisa and walked through the ruins of Pompei. We were able to view original paintings by some of my favorite artists, including Monet, and ate the most amazing pasta I have ever tasted. My favorite of all was driving the back roads through Tuscany, ending up in the picturesque hilltop town of Cortona. The movie *Under the Tuscan Sun* was filmed there, and it felt like we were in the movie as we experienced the magic of Tuscany.

Although I would stop fertility treatments for close to a year, motherhood was never far from my thoughts. Whether I was enjoying travel or staying busy with psychology papers and school assignments, I still was very aware of the absence I felt. I was about to receive a BA in psychology, but I would have traded it all to receive the title of "mom."

A few weeks after graduation, Jason and I offered to host our family's end-of-the-year holiday dinners and celebrations at our house. As family gathered, I considered the next steps in our infertility journey. I called my fertility doctor in December 2011 and made an appointment for January 5, 2012 to discuss more options. I asked many people to pray over this appointment just like I had done for previous appointments. Sometimes they would pray with us over the phone, but many times people physically gathered around us as they prayed. Every step we took regarding infertility procedures was bathed in prayer from multiple people. You may wonder why we did this. The Bible says, "For where two or three are gathered together in my name, there am I in the midst of them" (MATTHEW 18:20, KJV).

Jason and I have always believed this to be true. It doesn't mean God is not listening when just one person is praying. As Christians, we all know the importance of a personal prayer life with God. There are countless verses in Scripture where God calls individuals to pray. One of my favorite examples of an individual's persistence is found in Luke 18. Jesus told the parable of the persistent widow and urged us to always pray and not lose heart. He told of a widow who would not leave a certain judge alone. She needed justice over a matter, and she would not give up until he ruled in her favor. Jesus described this judge as unjust, neither caring for God nor this woman. However, her persistence wore the judge out to the point that he granted her request. Jesus said that if this unjust judge who cared for no one could have the capacity to grant a request, how much

❧

There is something to
be said about people
coming together— like-
minded, united in faith—
believing God can move
on behalf of His people.

❧

more will God move on behalf of His children who He loves with an immeasurable love?

Noah, Hannah, Daniel, Naomi, King David, and Moses are just a few examples of individuals who often prayed one-on-one to God and He moved on their behalf. An active prayer life is vital when it comes to a personal relationship with Christ. I, too, have prayed thousands of individual prayers throughout my forty-seven years of life regarding one thing or another. It is what has sustained me and given strength in my times of need. However, there is something to be said about people coming together— like-minded, united in faith—believing God can move on behalf of His people.

We all know from a practical standpoint there is strength in numbers. This concept is pointed out in Scripture as well:

> Two people are better off than one, for they can help each other succeed. If one person falls, the other can reach out and help. But someone who falls alone is in real trouble. Likewise, two people lying close together can keep each other warm. But how can one be warm alone? A person standing alone can be attacked and defeated, but two can stand back-to-back and conquer. Three

are even better, for a triple-braided cord is not easily broken. (ECCLESIASTES 4:9–12, NLT)

So again, we claimed the words of Jesus when He said, "For where two or three are gathered together in my name, there am I in the midst of them" (Matthew 18:20, KJV). Along with family and friends, we asked for prayers continually from pastors, congregations, coworkers, and acquaintances. I wanted prayers going up as we sought out medical advice.

As Jason and I sat across from our sweet doctor on January 5, we were filled with hope, yet still a bit nervous as we did not know if any other medical procedures would be an option for us. We felt at ease with him; he was a great listener and very sympathetic to our struggles. He was a man of faith as well, and although he was a very successful infertility doctor, he was quick to say there was only so much he could do and the rest was left to a Higher Power. He reminded us of the progress that was made the previous year in finding the right combo of medications that ultimately assisted in ovulation, something we didn't know was possible. After successfully ovulating and three failed artificial inseminations, he informed us the next logical step would be IVF (in vitro fertilization).

He explained to us that IVF is a medical procedure where an egg or eggs are fertilized by sperm in a test tube. If a healthy embryo or embryos come about through this process, then the next step would be an embryo transfer to my uterus to give the embryo a better chance at attaching to my uterine wall. I didn't fully understand the IVF process at the time. I knew it had been a controversial subject and needed to know exactly what would be taking place if we went this route. My husband and I believe in the sanctity of life, so I needed to make sure that nothing unethical would occur. The doctor explained that he believed in the sanctity of life as well and would only be attempting to help my body achieve the results that would have come about naturally if I wasn't experiencing infertility issues. He answered every question we had about the process, so we were fully aware of each step.

As I mentioned in earlier chapters, endometriosis, fibroid tumors, and cysts on my ovaries all contributed to a "hostile environment" for fertilization, making it very difficult for pregnancy to occur unassisted. In fact, endometriosis alone can cause adhesions that can prevent fertilization or implantation of an embryo to the uterine wall. I not only had endometriosis but also cysts, fibroid tumors, and hormone imbalance.

Although the medicine helped my body produce an egg, the egg would still have to be reached by sperm, be fertilized, and reach the uterus, where it needed to attach to the uterine wall.

Our doctor explained that IVF could possibly help us get past these obstacles. Egg retrieval and fertilization would occur outside my body, then the fertilized embryo would be placed in my uterus. However, even if there was a successful embryo transfer, our doctor could not make the embryo attach to my uterus. "That is left to a Higher Power," he said. We wholeheartedly agreed.

We believe God uses the minds and skills of doctors to assist with many aliments, including infertility. However, as qualified as our doctor was—one of the best in the country—and as wonderful as medical advances and procedures are, every life is given by our Creator.

We had a lot to think about after this consultation. We felt comfortable with the IVF procedure, but the cost seemed astronomical. As mentioned before, we had looked into adoption, but the cost had always been an issue, so we didn't proceed. Now we were faced with an even more complicated decision. Either route, adoption or IVF, was going to cost anywhere

❧

As qualified as our doctor
was— one of the best in the
country— and as wonderful
as medical advances and
procedures are, every life
is given by our Creator.

❧

from $20,000 to $30,000. It wasn't going to be easy, but we figured we could make it work if we cut back on extra spending and made covering this amount our highest priority.

We still had to choose though; what route would we take? Adoption or IVF? I was thirty-five years old. If we proceeded with adoption, there could be a two-year wait, but at least we would know we would have a child. If we tried a round of IVF, there were no guarantees it would work and we couldn't afford more than one round. But because of my age and my worsening symptoms, if I was going to try to conceive with IVF, it had to be then.

I felt like I was standing at a fork in the road and didn't know which way to turn. There was not an easy answer. I hit my knees and cried out to God for help. My heart was so heavy. I truly wanted whatever God wanted for us. If He wanted to place a baby in my arms through the wonderful world of adoption, then that's what I wanted. If He wanted to allow me to conceive and carry a child, then that's what I wanted. I just wanted Him to guide me. I knew He would, but my prayer during this time was more specific than I had ever prayed before in my life: "God, Your will be done; please help me. I don't know what to do. Please give me specific direction so there's no confusion."

And this is where our story changes.

God was on the move! My answer came soon after this prayer. My memory fails as to the exact timing, but within a week or so after I prayed, I was flipping through the Bible, preparing to read a nightly passage before I went to bed as I often do. As I was trying to get to the passage I had previously bookmarked, the Bible literally fell open to Isaiah 54: "Sing, barren woman, who has never had a baby. Fill the air with song, you who've never experienced childbirth!. . . Clear lots of ground for your tents!" (1–2, MSG).

In other words: Get ready! It's gonna happen!

This was my answer! I knew I would carry a child. I smiled from ear to ear; I laughed; I cried. I raised my hands in thanksgiving to God when I read those words. They seemed to jump off the page like they were written just for me. I was filled with joy and a peace only God can give. I knew now what we should do.

I told Jason what I had experienced, and he was thrilled! He agreed this was the answer we needed to proceed with IVF. The next afternoon, I was visiting with Jason's parents, and I read the passage to them. I told them I believed this was God's promise to me that

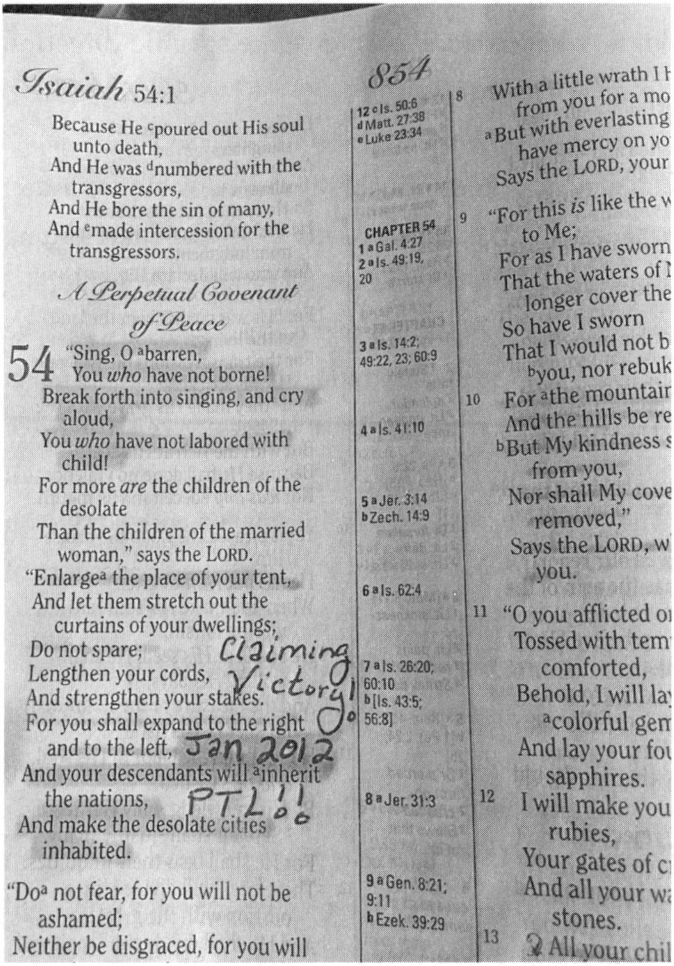

Isaiah 54:1   *854*

Because He cpoured out His soul
    unto death,
And He was dnumbered with the
    transgressors,
And He bore the sin of many,
And emade intercession for the
    transgressors.

*A Perpetual Covenant
of Peace*

54 "Sing, O abarren,
    You *who* have not borne!
Break forth into singing, and cry
    aloud,
You *who* have not labored with
    child!
For more *are* the children of the
    desolate
Than the children of the married
    woman," says the LORD.
2 "Enlargea the place of your tent,
And let them stretch out the
    curtains of your dwellings;
Do not spare;
Lengthen your cords,
And strengthen your stakes.
For you shall expand to the right
    and to the left,
And your descendants will ainherit
    the nations,
And make the desolate cities
    inhabited.

4 "Doa not fear, for you will not be
    ashamed;
Neither be disgraced, for you will

[handwritten: Claiming Victory Jan 2012 PTL!!]

[center cross-reference column:]
12 cIs. 50:6
dMatt. 27:38
eLuke 23:34

CHAPTER 54
1 aGal. 4:27
2 aIs. 49:19,
20

3 aIs. 14:2;
49:22, 23; 60:9

4 aIs. 41:10

5 aJer. 3:14
bZech. 14:9

6 aIs. 62:4

7 aIs. 26:20;
60:10
b[Is. 43:5;
56:8]

8 aJer. 31:3

9 aGen. 8:21;
9:11
bEzek. 39:29

8 With a little wrath I h
    from you for a mo
aBut with everlasting
    have mercy on yo
Says the LORD, your

9 "For this *is* like the w
    to Me;
For as I have sworn
That the waters of l
    longer cover the
So have I sworn
That I would not b
    byou, nor rebuk

10 For athe mountair
And the hills be re
bBut My kindness s
    from you,
Nor shall My cove
    removed,"
Says the LORD, w
    you.

11 "O you afflicted or
    Tossed with temi
    comforted,
Behold, I will lay
acolorful gen
And lay your fou
    sapphires.

12 I will make you
    rubies,
Your gates of c
And all your wa
    stones.

13 All your chil

IVF was going to work, so they should get ready to be grandparents. They were beyond excited. We all cried and thanked God for His direction. I told the others who had been praying for us to change their prayers.

You see, God had promised me I was going to carry a child, so there was no need to keep asking. I wanted all the prayers going up to change from asking God to thanking God in advance for what He was going to do for us.

As we started the IVF process, the goal was to get me to ovulate again and in a big way. Medicine was prescribed, and detailed instructions were given as to how and when I was to take the meds and administer hormone shots to overstimulate my ovaries. I won't expand on the how-tos of the ovulation process, but it is very specific and time sensitive. I was monitored closely by ultrasound to keep track of my progress so the doctor would know if and when to schedule an egg retrieval.

I was happy to find out my body responded well to the medicine and the staff was going to schedule my procedure. There was a lot weighing on the egg retrieval procedure. The doctor hoped to retrieve a high egg count to give us the best opportunity to get as many eggs as possible; it wasn't certain that all the eggs retrieved would be healthy. When I was researching the subject, I found on average there are ten to twenty eggs retrieved during most egg retrieval procedures, in many cases more than twenty. Again, we had a lot of people thanking God with us as I was about to go through this whole process, so I wasn't worried.

On February 20, 2012, as I lay on the table preparing for the egg retrieval, I prayed for God to have His way concerning the number of eggs retrieved. I thanked Him for what He was about to do.

As the doctor finished up, he said, "Well, Mrs. Mendenhall, we didn't get quite as many eggs as I was hoping for, but the procedure went well. We retrieved seven eggs."

"Is that enough?" I asked.

"Yes, we only need one!" he said with a smile. "We're looking for healthy eggs, of course, so although it's not necessarily a high egg count, I'm happy we have at least seven to look through."

Happy the retrieval went well, we went home and over the next few days waited for updates on the IVF process. The medical staff would oversee the next phase, which included fertilization of the healthy eggs with sperm in a laboratory setting. We received a call confirming two healthy embryos had formed! They sent us pictures of our two embryos and oh, what a beautiful sight it was to these tear-filled eyes! I didn't know if we would have two babies, but as I looked at the pictures, I did feel in my heart that I was looking at the beginning stage of at least one of my children. I proudly hung this picture on my refrigerator door and showed it off to family and friends when they'd stop by. I would walk past it in the kitchen and say, "Hi, little babies!"

I prayed over them and praised God for His continued guidance. There was no doubt in my mind that He was moving! From the scripture in Isaiah jumping off the pages just for me to the picture of our formed embryos on our refrigerator door, we were praising and God was moving!

Before I continue with the best part of our story, I want to take a moment to point out that the lessons we learned during this particular time in our lives continue to be life-changing principles we practice to this day. God has given us so many promises in His Word. They are promises He will keep! We are learning to stop asking for something He has already promised and simply start claiming those promises! How do we do this? By verbally thanking Him in advance for what He's about to do. Faith is not just believing in something we can't see. Faith is something we can practice. How do we practice faith? We "clear lots of ground for" our tents. We make preparations for what's about to take place before it happens. When it comes to

The lessons we learned
during this particular time
in our lives continue to be
life-changing principles
we practice to this day.
God has given us so many
promises in His Word. They
are promises He will keep!

God's promises, speak as though they are yours and you are currently enjoying them. Live as though you already have the answers. Speak as if the mountain has already moved!

≈

For assuredly, I say to you, whoever says to this mountain, "Be removed and be cast into the sea," and does not doubt in his heart, but believes that those things he says will be done, he will have whatever he says. (Mark 11:23)

Chapter 5

REVELATION

LTHOUGH WE HAD ORIGINALLY INTENDED TO have the next procedure, the embryo transfer, right away, minor sickness prevented me from proceeding on schedule. I, of course, needed to be as healthy as possible when undergoing such an important procedure, so we opted to postpone the transfer until I was feeling better. Although disappointing, it was necessary to have our two embryos frozen until I was recovered and could proceed with the transfer. In hindsight, it was God's perfect timing coming into fruition.

Two and a half months later, as we approached this final fertility procedure, we claimed God's promise to us in Isaiah 54 like never before. We had been trying to have a child for over nine years; five of those years assisted by several doctors. On May 4, 2012, the morning of the transfer, I opened my Facebook page and began to write:

> To all my FB friends who believe in the power of prayer, please, please, hold me up in prayer this morning and over the next few days. Jason and I have been seeing doctors trying to conceive for over five years with no success. This has been heartbreaking for us. Today I have the final procedure that will end our IVF process…the embryo transfer. We have two precious fertilized embryos being transferred, and we are trusting God that in about ten days our pregnancy test will be positive. I've been seeing fertility specialists for five years, but I need the Great Physician to intercede for us this morning! Please bombard heaven's door on our behalf! I'm praising God in advance for what He's about to do in our lives!

My phone began to ding with Facebook notifications:

"I'm praying for you…God is in control."

"I'm praying right now."

"Praying! Great is thy faithfulness, oh God my Father."

"Your post has touched my heart and I know God will reward your faithfulness! I am praying!!"

"God's Word promises that He will give us the desires of our heart. Praying and believing with you."

"Praying, praying, praying!!!! Looking forward to rejoicing with you!!"

"Our God is good all the time and your prayers have been heard. We BELIEVE this day God will deliver."

"I thought of you the moment I woke up today. You have my prayers!"

"There have been and will be many more prayers going up."

I believe these prayers from Facebook friends all over the country were reaching heaven! In addition to this social media post, several churches throughout the country were earnestly praying for this procedure. I again had asked those who had personally walked this infertility journey with us to be praying those prayers of thanksgiving in advance for what God was about to do. I can't emphasize enough how this concept of praising God in advance instead of just asking changed our lives!

When we arrived at the doctor's office, God gave us a peace that, like Scripture says, surpasses all under-standing. I was reminded of God's promise to me in Isaiah 54 and comforted by the words of Jesus in Mark 11:24: "Therefore I tell you, whatever you ask for in prayer, believe that you have received it, and it will be yours" (NIV). As I was led into the room where the transfer was to take place, I lay on the table knowing it was all in God's hands.

The procedure was explained to us and didn't take long at all. The doctor used a long, thin cath-eter containing our two embryos, along with a small amount of fluid. The catheter passed through my cervix and into my uterus, where our embryos were released. The doctor informed us all went well.

"I've now done all I can do that is medically possible. The rest is left to a Higher Power," he said once again.

～

I was reminded of God's
promise to me in Isaiah
54 and comforted by the
words of Jesus in Mark 11:24:
"Therefore I tell you, whatever
you ask for in prayer, believe
that you have received it, and
it will be yours." As I was
led into the room where the
transfer was to take place,
I lay on the table knowing
it was all in God's hands.

～

As we prepared to go home, our nurse came into our room with instructions explaining the last phase our fertility journey. We would now have to wait to see whether our embryos would attach to my uterus. She informed us that if the embryos were going to attach, they would do so within twelve to thirty-six hours. So I was given strict instructions to go home and rest for the next thirty-six hours.

"Put your feet up and have Jason spoil you for the next few days," she said. "Then, in ten days, take a pregnancy test. If your test is positive, call us and we will schedule blood work to be drawn to confirm a positive result. Don't take a test before the ten days have passed. It will do no good. Ten days from now will be the earliest the pregnancy hormone can be detected by either a pregnancy test or blood work here at the office. For now, just rest and try not to worry," she said.

We went home and did just that. I changed into my pj's and headed for the couch. Jason was his same sweet self and took good care of me, as always. He brought me a glass of juice, a plate of food, and made sure I was comfortable. We watched some news and settled in for the night. I was looking forward to getting a good night's sleep after a long day. I wouldn't know till morning just what a night it turned out to be!

I woke up the next morning around 8:30 a.m. I realized that I hadn't been up during the night to use the bathroom, like I usually do. I stretched out and rolled over, and there was Jason, still laying in the bed. This was unusual. He was normally up before me, already in the living room watching the news.

"Good morning, babe. Are you awake?" he asked.

"Yes, I'm awake," I replied.

What an unusual question that was; he could obviously see I was awake. But when I realized he had tears running down his face, I sat up quickly.

"What's wrong? Why are you crying? Are you okay?!" I asked.

"I'm okay," he said as he tried to reassure me. I didn't feel reassured, though. These were not just tears. His eyes were red and swollen from weeping.

"How are you feeling?" he asked me.

"I'm feeling fine, but you don't look fine! What is wrong?" I asked again.

"I'm okay, but I have to tell you something," he replied with tears still in his eyes.

"What is it?!" I questioned. I was so concerned.

There were many things going through my head in this short thirty-second interaction. I had just gone through one of the most important procedures of my life the day before, and now my husband was weeping in our bed, needing to tell me something. Was he nervous the procedure hadn't worked and we couldn't afford to try again? Did he learn of some kind of horrible news since last night? Did someone die? He could not tell me quick enough!

"What is it, babe?" I asked again urgently.

He looked at me, tears flowing. "Are you gonna think I'm crazy?" he asked.

"Of course not. What do you mean? What is it?" I replied.

"Babe, you're pregnant," he said in a soft voice, but in a very matter-of-fact way. "It worked. We're gonna have a baby."

"What?" I exclaimed.

Nearly ten years' worth of negative pregnancy tests flashed before my eyes. Even the thought this might possibly be true filled my eyes with tears immediately.

"What do you mean?" I asked. "The nurse just told us yesterday there's no way to know for ten days whether it worked or not."

"Oh, it worked," he assured me.

"Well, how do you know it worked? Did you have a dream or something? Did God confirm it to you in a dream that it worked?" I couldn't imagine what he meant.

"No," he said, shaking his head back and forth, crying, smiling. "It was definitely *not* a dream."

"What then? How do you know this?" I was hanging on every word.

"Are you sure you're not gonna think I'm crazy?" he asked for a second time.

"Babe, of course not. Tell me! How do you know this?" I couldn't wait one more second for him to explain.

To my amazement, he began to tell me about seeing the most incredible, life-changing event of our lives!

"There were angels in our room last night," he said. Tears falling, voice cracking, he could hardly get out what he had experienced.

"What?" I exclaimed. *My* tears were now flowing.

"Do you believe me?" he asked.

"Yes! Go on, tell me everything! What do you mean there were angels in our room? You saw them? What did they look like? What did they say? Did they tell you I was pregnant? Tell me everything!" I could hardly get my questions out fast enough.

Using handfuls of tissues to wipe his face, he told me what had happened. "I went to sleep last night like I normally do, nothing unusual. I woke up, startled, because I heard a noise. I was scared for a second,

"There were angels in our room last night," he said. Tears falling, voice cracking, he could hardly get out what he had experienced.

"What?" I exclaimed. My tears were now flowing.

"Do you believe me?" he asked.

"Yes! Go on, tell me everything!

because I thought maybe I had forgotten to set the alarm and someone had broken into our room, but in the length of time it took for that thought to cross my mind, the fear was gone and there was an immediate peace. I mean a peace like I had never felt before. All at once my fear was gone, and I knew exactly what was happening.

"I knew it was angels I was seeing and hearing as they made their way over to you. I knew they were there because God was answering our prayers. All I could do was fall on my knees beside the bed! It almost felt like an involuntary movement. I just fell down, my hands went up, and I began to worship God because I knew I was in His presence. I began to sing worship songs: "He Is Here," "Holy Ground," whatever came to mind as I worshiped and thanked Him for what He was doing."

"What was I doing during all this?" I exclaimed. "I didn't hear any of this!"

"You were just lying there, sleeping!" he replied. "I watched as they, three of them, made their way to your side of the bed and hovered over you. I was in absolute awe, and I wanted you to see them so badly, so I reached my hand over to you to try to wake you up. My fingers recoiled and my hand literally retracted back from you. I wasn't allowed to touch you. It wasn't a scolding but a definite 'you're not allowed to touch what is happening right now.' I immediately took my hand away and continued to stay on my knees by the bed. I never stood up any of the time. I only stayed on my knees.

"I continued to watch them. They were of human shape, but I could see no details of their faces. They didn't have wings, yet they hovered over you. They were tall, a cylindrical shape, and shined with a silvery glow. There was one other light directly over you. I don't know if it was another angel or not. If it was, its form wasn't as visible as the other three, who I knew for sure were angels. It was a bright light. It was higher up and farther from you. I didn't perceive this light to be God; I can only describe it as a fourth light that looked more like the shape of a star in the distance. When I say 'in the distance,' it was like a part of our ceiling was gone and I was looking up at the sky, but we were definitely all in our room! Of the three angels over you, the one in the middle would look up and then look down at you…look up and then look down at you, over and over. The two angels on each side of the one in the middle were just still, as though they were guarding or assisting the one in the middle.

"I remember thinking, *Wow, God, I can't believe You're doing this for us!*

"Then, although there were never any audible voices, there was immediate communication from the angels. They said, 'No, this is not happening just for you. This is how He does it every time.'

"Again, I didn't hear an audible voice or see lips moving, but it was a direct communication from them. There was absolutely no doubt they wanted me to know that distinction. What I was seeing was not just happening to you and for us. This was how it happens every time, for everyone!"

His tears kept flowing, as did mine.

He continued, "I watched as they hovered over you; then there were one, two, three, four flashes of light as they all disappeared one by one out of the room. Not long after, the sun began to rise and light flooded our room. It was peaceful and quiet. I got up from my knees, went into the bathroom to wash my face and clean up. I looked a mess. I was weeping, snottin', blowing my nose, in awe of what I had just witnessed. I came back into the room and have been laying here ever since waiting on you to wake up. I was pretty sure it was all over and finished, but after I experienced my hand drawing back from you, I didn't dare touch you or wake you up just in case."

He reached out his hand slowly and poked my arm. We both laughed as he said, "Okay, I guess it's all right now."

I, too, was in absolute awe. How do you wrap your mind around something so remarkable, literally supernatural? I wasn't surprised God answered our prayer, because we had been claiming He would, but I was completely taken back as to how He revealed it to us! The thought of angels hovering over me was enough to blow my mind, but the realization I was finally pregnant after all these years was almost too much to take. To top it all off, Jason was allowed to see it all and be the one to tell me I was pregnant before it was even medically possible to be detected by a pregnancy test or blood work. We held each other and cried. I put my hands over my belly and cradled it for the first time knowing there was a baby inside. Jason got down close to my belly and said, "Hello in there; this is your daddy!" That moment was truly spectacular and still to this day is hard to describe in words.

We continued to talk for probably close to two hours, just sitting in our bed. I asked him a million questions and tears continued to flow as he tried to explain what he had experienced.

"How long were they in our room?" I questioned.

"I'm not positive, but it felt like it was about forty-five minutes from the time I was awakened to the time the sun rose and it was all over," he replied.

"So you never heard any audible voices from them the whole time?" I asked.

"No," he said, "but they communicated with me, no doubt about it, just not with words. I could not see their mouths or any distinct details of their faces. I heard noise though. When they moved from where I was over to you, their movement sounded like a... *swoosh*. The only way I know how to describe it is, it sounded like the noise made when someone is wearing socks and scoots their feet along carpet. Although they did not seem to walk. It was like they floated over to you, then continued to hover over you. The sound as they moved reminded me of how some songwriters have described hearing 'the brush of angels' wings.' That's what it sounded like when they moved, although they had no wings. They were very bright. A silvery color. I was not fearful but remained reverent and knew to just stay kneeling. It was the most incredible thing I've ever seen.

"To top it all off, you're pregnant!"

I can't begin to express the joy we felt. After all our talking, we knelt by the side of our bed and I began to

❧

We wept as I thanked God
for not only answering
our prayers but also for
allowing Jason to see those
prayers being answered in
such a magnificent way!

❧

pray. We wept as I thanked God for not only answering our prayers but also for allowing Jason to see those prayers being answered in such a magnificent way!

How extraordinary to have experienced a literal glimpse of the psalmist's description:

≈

You created my inmost being; you knit me together in my mother's womb. I praise You because I am fearfully and wonderfully made; your works are wonderful, I know that full well. My frame was not hidden from you when I was made in the secret place, when I was woven together in the depths of the earth. Your eyes saw my unformed body; all the days ordained for me were written in your book before one of them came to be. (Psalm 139:13–16, NIV)

Chapter 6

FOR THIS CHILD
I PRAYED

AS WE WERE STILL ON OUR KNEES, MY PHONE rang. It was one of my best friends, Rita Beth. She had told me the day before she would call in the morning to check on me.

I looked at Jason and said, "It's Rita Beth. She's gonna want to know how I'm feeling. Are you okay with me telling her now? I mean we don't have proof yet from a pregnancy test."

Jason smiled and said, "Babe, you can tell whoever you want to tell. You're pregnant. No doubt about it!"

～

To hear the words "you're pregnant" from my husband— not from two lines on a pregnancy test; not from a doctor or nurse; but from my spouse who had walked this journey with me—was special on so many levels.

～

To hear the words "you're pregnant" from my husband—not from two lines on a pregnancy test; not from a doctor or nurse; but from my spouse who had walked this journey with me—was special on so many levels. He knew better than anyone else the pain I felt for nearly ten years from all the failed attempts. He also understood the joy I felt better than anyone else as it was revealed to us that we were finally pregnant.

Jason has never been a guy to announce to a group of people that he was "thinking" about doing something. He would wait until he had a plan and could see it was going to work before he would let anyone know. For instance, he told no one other than me and his parents that he might go to graduate school. He only told friends and extended family after he was enrolled, when it was actually happening. He was like this in every aspect of his life. Yet he excitedly told me to tell Rita Beth and anyone else I wanted that I was pregnant. He couldn't care less that we didn't have proof to show. He had been in the presence of God and that was all the proof he needed!

When I answered the phone, Rita Beth said, "Hey there! How are you feeling after your procedure?"

"Well," I said, "I gotta tell you something. Are you ready for this?"

"Sure!" she replied.

"It worked!" I exclaimed.

"What do you mean?" she asked.

"I'm pregnant!" I announced for the first time. "It's a crazy-sounding story, but Jason saw angels in our room last night and…" I proceeded to tell her the whole story.

She believed us immediately and was thrilled for us! We cried as I talked about the details and how amazing it all was. She, too, had struggled with infertility and knew the pain I had gone through. She had talked and prayed with me countless times through all those years, so it was special she was the first one I was able to tell. At the end of the conversation, she was her same cute self and said, "Wow! Well, okay! Congrats! And it's awesome we don't have to wait nine more days to find out if it worked!"

"Ha, yes!" I replied.

Her affirmation and belief this pregnancy was a done deal was a breath of fresh air for me and a testament to her faith as well!

Jason and I continued to tell our story to family and friends throughout the day. Everyone believed and rejoiced with us. There were a whole lot of tears and literal shouts of hallelujah over those phone calls.

We talked about every detail. My father-in-law speculated on what the angel in the middle was doing when he looked up and then back down at me, over and over again.

"Can you imagine what was taking place?" he said. "Was the angel looking up to the heavens, listening for instructions, then looking back down at you, assisting God somehow? Maybe he was being the hands of God as your baby attached and was knit into your womb?" he continued.

We don't have the answers for everything Jason saw, but everything about it was beautiful, miraculous, and very specific. We still contemplate what it all meant to this day.

The God-wink in this story is the date when I should have taken a pregnancy test. Remember, the nurse had told me to wait ten days after the procedure before taking a test or getting blood work. When I looked at the calendar and counted ten days, it was, drum roll please, Mother's Day! If that wasn't orchestrated by God, I don't know what is! How special is that?! How specific is that?! This is just one of the many ways throughout this story that I felt like I got a big ol' hug and wink from God. It was a reminder that He does give us the desires of our hearts in His timing, and in an even more extraordinary

~

When I looked at the calendar and counted ten days, it was, drum roll please, Mother's Day! If that wasn't orchestrated by God, I don't know what is! How special is that?! How specific is that?! This is just one of the many ways throughout this story that I felt like I got a big ol' hug and wink from God.

~

way than maybe we were expecting. As Ephesians 3:20 states, "God is able to do exceedingly abundantly above all we can ask or think."

The same evening after our miraculous visit, I got on social media and told our story. We wanted to share the miracle with as many people as possible before we had actual proof from a test. It was testament to the fact we knew beyond a shadow of a doubt that God had performed this miracle, not the IVF procedure. IVF and our wonderful doctor assisted us, but none of it would have worked unless God ordained life into existence, and we wanted Him to get all the glory.

May 5, 2012

For everyone who has been praying for Jason and me, God has heard our cry! Our embryo transfer was yesterday morning, and although we are not due to take a pregnancy test until May 14, God came on the scene early this morning and bore witness to us that without a doubt we are pregnant! The story of what happened is so amazing and details too numerous to list on Facebook, but please join us in praising Him for our miracle! We have no doubt that right now I'm carrying a child… or two!

Comments started to pour in:

"Praise the Lord!"

"I am weeping with joy and praising our God!!"

"Praise Him. Our God is an Awesome God!!!! Thank you, Father. I'm so happy for you."

"Oh GL! You've made my day! Congratulations! What a meaningful Mother's Day this will be for you! God is so faithful!"

"Well, now I wanna know what happened!"

"God is so good to give us the desires of our hearts. I think He loves to surprise us. God bless you and your family."

"Praise the Lord for answered prayers."

"Praise God from Whom All Blessings Flow!!!
We Serve A Great And Awesome God who
has already answered our family's prayers.
So happy for you both and can't wait for your
precious gift to arrive."

"This is an awesome witness. Thank you Lord."

Most everyone's comments indicated they believed immediately. The Spirit bore witness to them that it was done. No test was needed to confirm. They not only believed our story because they knew and believed us, but they believed in the power of prayer and knew from experience that God still performs miracles in a big way. These comments truly encouraged us and further confirmed our belief there is strength in numbers. God promised that if His people, called by His name, would humble themselves and pray, seeking His face, He would answer them. God's children bombarded heaven on our behalf, and He heard and answered them. He honored our prayers as we stepped out in faith. We praised Him in advance for what He was about to do, and it was done! Praise His name!

I'll gently bring up that not all believed, however. They hoped it was true, but they understandably couldn't be certain. After all, we had no positive pregnancy test, and they didn't experience what we did in that room. I point this out only to emphasize that a supernatural encounter with God, as we experienced, leaves no doubt or confusion. An encounter with Him is life-changing and precise. It doesn't matter that it defies medical protocols. If God does it, it just is!

That same week, I went to my pastor and shared the good news that I was pregnant. He was delighted! He and his wife had prayed many years for us. I explained how we didn't have proof from a pregnancy test, but we knew the test would be positive on Mother's Day. He believed immediately! I asked him if I could speak during the service on Mother's Day to share the story with the congregation and bring my positive test to show the proof. He said absolutely. He hadn't even heard the details of the story yet, but he enthusiastically added me to the service schedule to share the news. He knew God had done something wonderful!

Knowing I would be taking the test in a few days, I went home and made sure I had pregnancy tests in my bathroom cabinet. Sure enough, I had three boxes. This was not surprising. I can't begin to guess just how many pregnancy tests I took over the course of almost ten years. I bought tests in bulk and always had them in my cabinet. Anytime my body felt the slightest difference, I would check. My monthly cycles were so abnormal I might take a test several times in a month. If I was nauseous, I'd test. If I felt light-headed, I'd test. If my hair felt thicker, I'd test. As unreasonable, and in some ways funny, as it may sound to have tested so much, it was actually really sad. Sad because as many times as I tested, literally hundreds of times, I never did get used to seeing that negative sign. It was always devastating, always disappointing, always exhausting.

So you can imagine how utterly excited I was to be taking this test on Sunday, May 14, 2012! It is a day I will never forget! I can't put into words how I felt knowing the pregnancy test I was about to take was going to be positive and I would actually see it with my eyes for the first time!

I woke up Sunday morning and went into the bathroom immediately. I opened all three boxes and laid them on the counter. I decided I might as well use all of them since they were there. I excitedly hollered for Jason to come in and we watched as one, two, three pregnancy tests turned positive for the first time in my life! We hugged, cried, and I squealed with excitement!

Although we were thrilled to be looking at the positive tests, I realized all three tests were from the dollar store and a bit difficult to read. Remember, I was getting ready to go to church, tell the story, and show off the test to everyone. I wanted to have a test that showed a big positive sign so it could be seen easily. So I sent my sweet husband off to Walmart to get another pregnancy test for me while I continued to get ready for church.

Well, a typical man for you here (*wink*)—he was not prepared for the wide array of pregnancy test options available and was a little overwhelmed. He wasn't sure which one to get, so he bought two big boxes for me to choose from. He came home and held up the boxes in front of me.

"This test will show a big plus sign and this test will show the written word 'positive.' I didn't know which one you'd prefer, so I got both," he said.

I smiled and thanked him. When I opened the two boxes, there were two tests in each of the boxes, so four tests all together. Again, I decided I might as well use all of them. I laid the four tests down on the bathroom countertop by the other three and we watched as all four of them turned positive! I got out my camera and took a picture of this beautiful sight. One, two, three, four, five, six, seven pregnancy tests and every one positive! We knew they would be, but the joy to see our faith become sight was indescribable.

Observant readers will notice that, again, the number seven showed up. This was the second time the number seven showed up, but it was the first time I took note. I thought to myself for a split second, *Hmm, seven eggs and now seven pregnancy tests.*

I continued to get ready for church but tucked the fact that this was the second time the number seven showed up in the back of my mind.

As we made our way to church that morning, we were filled with excitement. Under most circumstances, I dread public speaking. Singing in front of a crowd doesn't bother me, but speaking always has. However, I was so excited to share what had happened to us that I couldn't wait to get up and speak. I shared our story, and the Holy Spirit moved in our service in such a sweet way. When I was done telling the story, I sang one of the worship songs Jason had sung as he fell to his knees when first realizing there were angels in our room. Jason stood to his feet in the service that Mother's Day morning, arms up in praise as I sang "He is Here" written by Kirk Talley.

It was so special to see my mom, who had prayed countless prayers over me, with arms upraised, thanking God for answered prayers for her daughter on her first Mother's Day. Jason's dad shouted out, "Thank You, God," and his mother cried tears of joy.

There were shouts of praise and claps of thanksgiving to God all over the sanctuary for answering the prayers of our congregation. What an extraordinary day! It is one we will never forget.

The next day we informed our fertility doctor and staff of my positive result. They were thrilled! I scheduled a follow up appointment for blood work to be drawn at my ob-gyn's office in Meridian, Mississippi. My ob-gyn would once again be taking over my care. He, too, as well as staff from his office, were so very excited for us! He was smiling from ear to ear when he heard the news of my positive result.

As the days turned into weeks, I was experiencing all the joys of pregnancy I had longed to experience for so many years. I started reading up again on anything pregnancy related—healthy food, healthy exercise, maternity clothes, and nursery items. Even the first couple of weeks of nauseousness was exciting in a weird way. It was a symptom of pregnancy, so there was no way I could feel upset about it. Jason spoiled me rotten all the time. He made sure I wasn't overdoing it and helped any way he could. He helped with housework and brought me ginger ale when I was nauseous and tacos when I started to feel better.

We couldn't wait for the first ultrasound, not only to see the first pictures but to find out if we were having one baby or two! I asked my doctor when I could have my first ultrasound, and he let me know that the earliest we could have one would be when I was between six to eight weeks pregnant. "We'll have the nurse look at our clinic's available appointments and see when we can get you scheduled during that time frame," he said.

When I was at the appointment desk, I enthusiastically told the scheduler when I would be six weeks pregnant, hoping to get my ultrasound as soon as possible.

"I'm so sorry," she said. "We are booked solid that week. We can get you in the next week, though, when you're seven weeks."

There was that seven again! This was becoming very intriguing.

"I'll take it!" I replied.

Those next several weeks of waiting for the appointment seemed like several months! Finally, the time had come. Unfortunately, Jason was out of town working, but he could not wait to hear all about it. I missed him being there for sure, but I was thrilled to be going to an ultrasound, this time knowing it would be a joyous occasion. Most of my ultrasounds over the years had been because I was having pain or needed to monitor infertility issues. Not this time though! I was about to see our baby.

My sonographer was so sweet and shared her excitement over what we were about to see and find out. As she turned the monitor toward me, I scanned the screen intently. I teared up as she pointed and said, "Here's your baby! There is one, not two. Everything looks perfect!"

"Oh my word!" I exclaimed. "This is amazing!" I cried as I took it all in. It was the most precious moment.

"And you're sure there's not another baby in there, hiding behind the other one, right?" I had just read a story of that happening, so I had to ask.

She smiled. "No, I'm sure there's just one. Are you okay with that? Are you disappointed?" she asked.

"No," I replied. "I mean we've thought about how neat it would be to have a multiple pregnancy, but I can't even begin to explain to you the joy I'm feeling right now! I've wanted to look at an ultrasound monitor and see a baby on this screen for almost ten years. I could not be happier!"

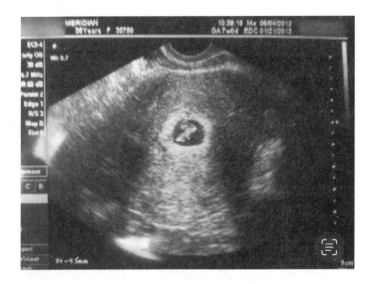

As the weeks turned into months, I continued to thank God for answering our prayer. I shared our remarkable story often as acquaintances continued to hear of my pregnancy.

At fourteen weeks I had a 4D ultrasound and found out we were having a girl! We were tickled pink! And so was her nursery. It was painted a neutral tan with a pink flower mural covering choice sections of the walls. White satin curtains framed the window, a beautiful crystal chandelier hung from the ceiling, and her Victorian-style crib was filled with pink fluffy blankets. Her closet was filled with adorable ruffled outfits and big matching hair bows from grandmas, aunties, and friends. It seemed we were preparing for a princess! It was such a joyful time in our lives.

As my pregnancy neared its end, I found out I would need to deliver by C-section to avoid some minor complications. I was given a due date of January 28, but that changed to January 21. As I got closer to my due date, during a routine examination, my doctor said, "Well, she's not gonna need to stay in there as long as I originally thought, so I've rescheduled your C-section for January 7."

Well, of course you did! I thought, smiling with excitement. *It's a seven, after all.*

I couldn't wait to get home to tell Jason. Not only did we get to meet her two weeks earlier than expected, but her birthday would be on the seventh!

Since that day—January 7, 2013—McKenzie Brooke Mendenhall has been our one and only, the joy of our lives! She was born at 10:47 a.m., weighing in at eight pounds three ounces.

She initially had dark curly hair that quickly changed to light blonde within just a few weeks. Our little blue-eyed girl was dramatic from the very beginning, showing her personality in her first hospital photo the very day she was born. The nurse came back holding the hospital picture and said, "Look, she's blowing a kiss!"

Her right hand was positioned close to her face and her little lips were puckered as though she were kissing the world hello!

Little did we know at the time how well this photo would depict her characteristics to this day. Her zest for life is evident. Now ten years old, she loves to sing, draw, paint, and read. We all love to travel, and this is where we have seen her adventurous spirit thrive. Wherever the location, she seamlessly acclimates to

her surroundings; whether hiking, snorkeling, skiing, parasailing, or zip-lining, she's fearless.

She has an enormous sense of humor as well; not a day goes by that Jason and I don't experience a laugh-out-loud moment from her shenanigans. We are most proud of her tender heart. She often asks if we can call or visit our elderly neighbors or those we've heard are sick to see if there's anything we can do for them. We believe God has placed within her, like He does all of us, exactly what she needs to make this world a better place. We thank God for her every day and pray He uses her in a mighty way throughout her life.

≈

For this child I prayed, and the LORD has granted me my petition which I asked of Him. (1 SAMUEL 1:27)

Chapter 7

A WINK AND A HUG

OD'S GUIDING HAND CONTINUED TO SHOW UP through the number seven with what I call *God winks*. Squire Rushnell, a *New York Times* bestselling author, coined the term "Godwinks" in his book *When God Winks*, which was the first in a series of ten books he's completed on this subject matter. This terminology was a great way to describe how I felt when we kept coming across the number seven throughout our story. I visualized God looking down, giving me a wink and a hug, and saying, "Yep, that was Me. I did that for you. I made that happen. I opened that door." The

❧

I visualized God looking
down, giving me a wink
and a hug, and saying, "Yep,
that was Me. I did that for
you. I made that happen.
I opened that door."

❧

number seven is now, obviously, our family's favorite number. McKenzie often smiles when she hears the number seven being talked about in a sermon or discovers the number seven has been used in some practical way throughout the day. It's her number, our number—such a special part of our lives now.

Having grown up in church, I knew enough about the number seven to take notice when it started showing up throughout our story. I remembered it being called God's number, but I didn't really know why, other than the obvious reason: God created the earth in six days and rested on the seventh. I recently started looking into the significance of numbers throughout Scripture and found that not only the number seven but numbers in general during biblical times were often used to symbolize a greater meaning.

The number seven was symbolic in ancient culture and literature. It is used throughout Scripture more than 700 times. If we include *seventh* or *sevenfold*, that number goes up to over 850 references. It is typically used to depict completion and perfection, both spiritually and physically, as well as healing and fulfillment of promises.

Here are a few of many examples:

- God created the world in six days, and upon completion He rested on day seven (Genesis 2).
- When asked how many times to forgive, Jesus said, "Seventy times seven" (Matthew 18:22).
- In the Old Testament we find that the Israelites were to cancel all debts made to each other on every seventh year (Deuteronomy 15).
- In 2 Kings 5, Naaman the leper was told to dip in the Jordan seven times and he was cleansed of his leprosy.
- God promised Joshua the walls of Jericho would fall if he and his army marched once a day, every day, for six days, and then seven times on the seventh day. The walls fell when Joshua obeyed (Joshua 6)!
- After the flood, a rainbow made up of seven visible colors symbolized a promise that God would never again overtake the earth with such great waters (Genesis 9).
- In Proverbs 9 we find the house of Wisdom is set on seven pillars. These seven pillars are knowledge, discretion, the fear of the Lord, counsel, instruction, understanding, and reproof. With the number seven symbolizing

Our First Valentine's Day, February, 1998.

May 1999

Deployment Homecoming Lemoore, California

Meridian, MS

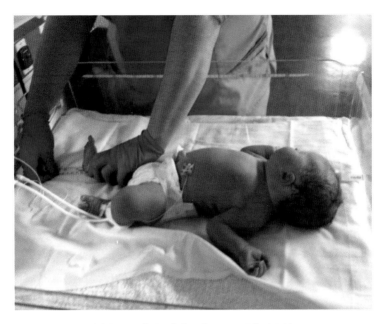

McKenzie's Birthday, January 7th, 2013

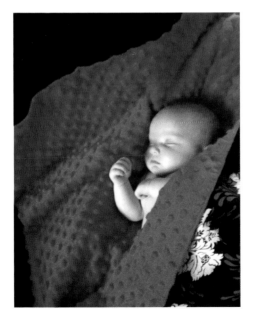

Seven Weeks Old

Nine Months Old

One and-a-Half Years Old

Two Years Old

Three Years Old

At Work With Dad

Kindergarten Graduation, Five Years Old

Seven Years Old

Nine Years Old

Ten Years Old

Our Traditional "Everybody Act Crazy" Picture!

completeness, this is a beautiful description of Wisdom's house, which is unmovable.

- In Revelation alone, the number seven is used fifty-four times, describing end-of-the-world prophecy as John wrote letters to seven churches in Asia.
- Even from a practical standpoint, our world functions and works around a seven-day calendar week.

As I've studied more in depth, it has become so special to us to see the number seven used in our story so many times. The symbolic meanings of perfection, healing, fulfillment of promises, and completion could not be more relevant to our situation. Regarding perfection, and to recap what was mentioned in chapter 6, the first time I noticed the number seven in our story was during the egg retrieval. The doctor was hoping for a large amount of eggs to give us the highest chance at getting a good number of healthy eggs. When only seven were harvested, it was not what the doctor had hoped for. Nevertheless, it was perfect! It was a reminder that when God is a part of something He is never hindered by our circumstances. It always makes me smile when I look back and realize God took the time to manifest His guiding hand in this way; a wink and a hug showing me He was in control of this IVF process.

I also believe the seven eggs symbolized healing for me. My ob-gyn's opinion was I had probably never ovulated in my entire life. The very fact I was able to ovulate and have a successful egg retrieval is a beautiful example of how God uses medical professionals, advances in medicine, and medical procedures as a form of healing. He obviously is the One who created the minds of every man and woman that found these medical solutions, so I always give God the ultimate praise for medical advances. He showed His healing hand in a beautiful way, I believe, by allowing seven eggs to be harvested.

Next, I believe our seven positive pregnancy tests symbolized promises fulfilled. When I prayed for guidance about which route I should take, adoption or IVF, God answered very specifically through Isaiah 54. When I read "Sing, barren woman, you who never bore a child.... Enlarge the place of your tent" (NIV), I knew this was His promise to me that I would carry a child through IVF. He did indeed keep His promise

I always give God the ultimate praise for medical advances. He showed His healing hand in a beautiful way, I believe, by allowing seven eggs to be harvested.

to me, beautifully symbolized by seven positive pregnancy tests!

From seven healthy eggs to the promise kept and symbolized by the seven pregnancy tests, to the completion of that promise on her birth date of January 7, God's handiwork kept showing up!

As I began to do my research to write this book, I decided to look back over the years to see whether the number seven had showed up any more throughout our infertility journey. To my complete surprise, our infertility story from start to finish has been laden with the number seven. I took out a piece of paper and began to write down information starting from the moment Jason and I met. I was taken back in a way I can't express.

- Jason and I met in 1997.
- In 2003, we started trying for a baby. Jason and I both turned twenty-seven years old that year.
- After numerous moves with the navy, in 2007 we moved back to Mississippi, where our miracle eventually happened. At that time Jason joined Training Squadron Seven.
- During our IVF process there were seven eggs harvested from the egg retrieval.

- Angels were present as God answered our prayer on May 5, a Saturday, the seventh day of the week.
- Although not planned, we ended up taking seven pregnancy tests on Mother's Day … seven visual positive confirmations of what we already knew.
- McKenzie's first ultrasound was scheduled at seven weeks.
- McKenzie was born on January 7 at 10:47 a.m.
- McKenzie was born in the year 2013, the year Jason and I both turned thirty-seven.
- Although we originally planned to settle in Mississippi long term, circumstances required a change. We moved from Mississippi to Indiana in 2017, where Jason was transitioning from the navy to civilian flying.
- We moved to Tennessee in July (the seventh month) of 2020, when McKenzie was seven years old. I felt a huge pull to move to Tennessee even though it was during the pandemic and didn't seem like the greatest time to be moving. Now I know why I felt that pull. After the move, I started to feel an urgency about getting our story out. God was unfolding

a plan. We're surrounded here by specific people God is using to help make this book and future upcoming projects a reality.

- Tennessee is the seventh state I've lived in!

Y'all, you can't make this stuff up! I wrote all this down and saw a timeline perfectly orchestrated by God from the beginning of our journey, all for the purpose of it being told. We believe that the number seven was used at specific times and in specific ways—all to show God's guidance throughout our journey.

We have always sought God's guidance concerning every move—in careers, location, large purchases, and so on—and He has led us, so this concept isn't surprising. However, when I wrote down the timeline of our lives and saw how specifically He guided us, it was sobering.

Jason and I don't believe God guided us and answered our prayer only for us to receive our miracle. We believe He answered supernaturally and showed His handiwork specifically, to show the importance of the message the angels brought to us all. Alongside my role as a mother, sharing this story is the purpose of my life.

≈

When you realize God's purpose
for your life isn't just about you,
He will use you in a mighty way.

Dr. Tony Evans

Chapter 8

HOPE AND
HALLELUJAHS

N 2021, I STARTED FEELING AN URGENCY TO write down our story. I told Jason what was on my heart, and he agreed it was time. We have shared our story with churches, family, friends, acquaintances, and even strangers in the years since McKenzie's birth in January 2013. However, we've always felt there would come a time we would share it with a larger audience.

I think God allowed us to just be mom and dad for a season. We have gotten to witness our beautiful baby grow into a lovely ten-year-old girl. We have told McKenzie the story of that early morning miracle many times. In December of 2021, I told her it was now time to share what God has done for us with even more people. She was very excited and realized the importance of sharing what we've experienced.

I haven't felt an urgency like this about anything else in my life. Why the urgency? I believe there are many reasons. To start with, infertility affects millions of people worldwide, both women and men suffer. Research shows that infertility can cause depression and anxiety, leaving those involved feeling hopeless. It takes a tremendous toll on women's bodies. The physical pain and exhaustion from it all can be overwhelming. Likewise, spouses, children, parents, siblings, and friends can feel helpless to know how to comfort and support the woman and men in their life going through it.[*]

Jason and I pray our story gives hope to those going through infertility right now. That hope is to know life comes from a Creator who has a specific time for every person on this planet. When we were struggling, I just

---

[*] Jenny Lin and Leah Susser, "Recognizing the Psychological Toll of Infertility in Women," *Anxiety and Depression Association of America*, July 27, 2022, https://adaa.org/learn-from-us/from-the-experts/blog-posts/professional/recognizing-psychological-toll-infertility.

⚬

Jason and I pray our story gives hope to those going through infertility right now. That hope is to know life comes from a Creator who has a specific time for every person on this planet.

⚬

assumed my physical issues were the main contributing factor to my being unsuccessful at becoming pregnancy. However, looking back, my opinion is very different. No doubt my physical ailments were seen as obstacles of human conception. Looking at the big picture, the fact is, it wasn't God's timing for our daughter to be brought into this world. When it was His timing, there was nothing that could prevent her arrival!

The fact that we had two embryos transferred into my uterus and only one attached is another beautiful example that life is in God's hands alone. The fertility medicine helped me ovulate. The medical procedures helped procure two embryos. The fertility doctor assisted with placing both of them into my uterus. Both embryos went through the same fertility process. However, only one attached. This is because life is not just a biological process. Life exists when God ordains it to be.

So hold on! God's timing is everything! If you are meant to be parents, it will happen in His time and in His way. His way may be conceiving naturally, or like our case, through IVF. It may be through the beautiful process of adoption or foster care. These are the traditional means of becoming parents. But sometimes our desires are fulfilled by God in a way we may have never imagined for ourselves. Maybe God is calling you to an honorary role as a "second" mom or dad to a child or family. Maybe you will be asked to be a godparent. Maybe your role as an aunt or uncle will make a world of difference in a child's life. Whatever the role, if you truly seek God's direction for your life and desire His will above your own, He will fulfill the desire of your heart. How do I know this? Because His Word promises us He will.

Psalm 37:4 says, "Delight yourself in the LORD, and he will give you the desires of your heart" (ESV). That's a short verse, but oh, how powerful! It is a promise. He *will* give you the desires of your heart. In other words, the longing you may be feeling in your heart right now will be fulfilled, even if the fulfilling of those desires are not how you originally thought or prayed they'd be fulfilled. When God's plan comes together for you, you'll look back to find it was better than you could have imagined for yourself.

Ephesians 3:20 says, "Now all glory to God, who is able, through his mighty power at work within us, to accomplish infinitely more than we might ask or think" (ESV). Or as the New King James Version puts it, "Who is able to do exceedingly abundantly above

❧

Although I had to wait for what seemed like to me an enormous amount of time, during the wait God was orchestrating the most incredible masterpiece. Sharing the story of this masterpiece has turned out to be one of the greatest purposes of my life.

❧

all that we ask or think." This verse reminds us God not only knows the desires of our hearts, but He also understands them in a way we ourselves don't fully comprehend. He is able to fulfill those desires we asked for more infinitely, more abundantly, and exceedingly more than we ever even thought possible.

I desired a baby ten years before His fulfillment of that desire. Ten years is a long time: a decade, 120 months, 3,650 days. If it were up to me, I would have been pregnant immediately; I mean, who wants to be longing for something for ten years?! I certainly didn't. The wait was extremely difficult. The plan I desired for myself was not God's ultimate plan, however. Although I had to wait for what seemed to me like an enormous amount of time, during the wait God was orchestrating the most incredible masterpiece. Sharing the story of this masterpiece has turned out to be one of the greatest purposes of my life.

My desire for a child was fulfilled in a far grander way than I had asked for or could have even imagined it would be fulfilled. This one thing I know: when your husband sees angels in your room and tells you you're pregnant before it's medically possible to be detected, it puts a whole lot of things into perspective. Mainly this: God's got us! Hallelujah! We can rest assured He has a story perfectly written for our lives! He is the author of our story, though. When we try to write our own story, we'll get it wrong every time. I pray for everyone reading right now that you'll allow Him to write your story. Let Him lead, and you follow; the outcome—and the timing of that outcome—will be right every time.

We also pray our story encourages and renews the hearts of believers worldwide. If we can grasp the concept that God still works miracles in supernatural ways, it would change our generation! He still sends angels down from heaven! As believers, we never doubted it was possible to experience a supernatural encounter or miracle. We believed the stories in the Bible documenting angel interactions and miraculous events. We believed nothing was impossible for Him. When we experienced it ourselves, however, even our previous perception of God and who He is changed forever. To be a recipient of a heavenly encounter makes it impossible to ever again put limitations on His power! You are forever changed; likewise, those around you who hear of these miracles will be changed.

So, if you've ever experienced it, tell it! We need to share these important encounters and miracles. We need to tell others when God meets any kind of need in our lives, great or small. That's how the next generation and the ones after will know of Him. That's how they'll know there is hope in this world that very often seems hopeless. Let's tell how absolutely nothing is impossible with Him and only because of Him!

We also pray our story brings healing and hope to those who have suffered miscarriage and infant death. We realize our story may bring up more questions than we have answers for. You may ask *why*, as we did. *Why* would God go to such great lengths to send down angels from heaven as God placed a soul and knit your baby together in your womb, only to have that precious life end just weeks or a few short months later? *Why* would God allow your baby to grow for nine months, only for his or her life to end a few days after birth? *Why*? It seems cruel, doesn't it?

I've heard story after story from so many women— some dear friends, some strangers. All with similar yet very different stories. All suffered tremendous pain from such great loss, yet each one had an experience, setting, and scenario uniquely their own. Some miscarried unexpectedly. Some had a D&C after an ultrasound revealed no heartbeat. Some women had a great support system around them to help them through.

Some were treated as though their miscarriage was no big deal by friends, family, or medical staff. *"It happens all the time. You can try again." "Don't be sad. This is your body's way of getting rid of malformed fetuses." "You'll most likely pass your 'tissue' in the toilet."*

My precious friend, and so many women like her, explained to me how "passing tissue," as the experience is commonly called in medical facilities, is heart-wrenching. *My tissue*, they thought; but oh, it was so much more! It was their child who they already saw in their mind's eye. They had such high hopes and future dreams. This child was already deeply implanted in their heart, already loved and sometimes already named. They were expected to flush it down the toilet and just go on with their day. These women, ten, fifteen years later, still cry as they share their stories.

Some women carried their babies with no complications but delivered them stillborn. Some carried their child full-term, knowing their child would be stillborn or live for only a matter of hours or days. I can't possibly list all the different scenarios women and family members have endured. Again, some had a great support system, but some did not.

Often, on top of the grief from such great loss, some have had to endure well-meaning people's attempts of speaking comfort, which many times have only added to their pain:

"I'm so sorry for your loss. God must have needed another angel in heaven." "Aw, your baby is another flower in God's garden."

During this tremendous pain, comments about how "common" miscarriage is or how your baby is better off and must have been needed in heaven, make it incredibly hard not to feel alone in your mourning.

My sweet friends, and every reader who has had similar experiences, I can't tell you I have all the answers you need. I could easily be seen by some as just another failed attempt at trying to bring comfort. However, I pray our story in some way contributes to your healing. After what Jason and I experienced, we have no doubt that your child, although their life ended in miscarriage, stillbirth, or infant death, was indeed ordained by God for a specific purpose.

Scripture states there is indeed "a time for everything, and a season for every activity under the heavens: a time to be born and a time to die" (Ecclesiastes 3:1–2, NIV). There is a specific time God ordains life in the womb (Psalm 139:16). Some lives both begin and end in the womb. Some children are born and here for what seems to be an extraordinarily short amount of time. Some live what's considered to be long, full lives. We know from Scripture that every life has a number of days assigned that is known only to God (Job 14:5). There are no concrete answers explaining why one life ends at eight weeks and another life ends at eighty years old. But while we're here on earth, we see through a glass dimly and will see clearly only when we are one day united face-to-face with God and get the answers from Him (1 Corinthians 13:12). However short a life, however long a life, it is inevitable in this world that all life will end. I believe the key here is understanding there is a difference in the timetable of this world and the eternal world.

I read a simple yet profound statement not long ago on a social media post that is like-minded to my thoughts on this subject: "One day we'll close our eyes to time and open them to eternity." When we only think in terms of our time here on this earth, life will more often than not seem too short. But the reality is that we were not created for this present life only. God creates each life for a specific purpose, and that purpose is not limited by earth's timetable. God places an eternal soul within every life He creates; that soul lives on into the next eternal life. If we focus on life being lived only on this earth, it can be very confusing as to why God would take time to send down angels and ordain a life, only to take that life a short time later. It can make God seem like some great, big cruel being who gives life and just wants to show He can take it away whenever He pleases. Some can mistakenly feel God is doing this to somehow punish them or to test their strength.

This is not true. God's thoughts toward us are not evil but of hope and peace (Jeremiah 29:11). On the night my husband and I experienced this supernatural heavenly event, our room was filled with the indescribable love and almighty power of God as our daughter's life was handcrafted for a specific time and purpose. Jason could not even stand as he witnessed the powerful scene, yet he explained how he has never felt such love and peace at the same time. The beginning of life is specifically designed by a compassionate God who takes great joy in creating His most valuable of all creations.

Angels are present, ushering in His presence, as life is created. It is a truly remarkable experience. Jason was filled with awe as it was made known to him that this is the way all life comes to be. All life! If you have lost a child through miscarriage, your baby was no "tissue" being flushed down the toilet. Your child went

❧

The beginning of life is specifically designed by a compassionate God who takes great joy in creating His most valuable of all creations.

❧

through the same heavenly experience as our daughter. Although your child lived a short period of time on this earth, there was a specific purpose God had for your child. No matter the age when taken from this earth—eight months or eight years old—rest assured that your children are in perfect peace, fulfilling the purpose for which God intended, and you have the hope of reuniting with them someday.

―

Therefore my heart is glad, and my glory rejoices;
my flesh also will rest in hope.

PSALM 16:9

Chapter 9

NO MATTER THE CIRCUMSTANCE

THE HEARTBREAK OF INFERTILITY, MISCARRIAGE, and infant death; as well as encouragement of the church, are all important reasons writing this book was on my heart. However, to get down to the core of why I felt an urgency to get our story out, I will go back to the part of the story when the angels were in our room and were hovering over me. Jason said, "As I looked at the angels hovering over you, I remember thinking, *Wow, God, I can't believe You're doing this for us!*"

❧

You are of infinite value.
When God ordained your life,
like He did our daughter's on
the morning of May 5, 2012,
it, too, was a heavenly act.

❧

But he was immediately corrected. Jason heard no audible voice, nor did he see the angels' mouths moving, but they communicated this to him.

"No, this is not happening *only* for you. This is how He does it *every time*."

This communication from the angels is the main reason we are doing all we can to get this story out. This message is for everyone. You have a Creator!

You are of infinite value. When God ordained your life, like He did our daughter's on the morning of May 5, 2012, it, too, was a heavenly act. My words fail to describe how magnificent an event your arrival was. God stopped what He was doing, opened the windows of heaven, and sent down angels as He, the Creator of all things, knit you together in your mother's womb. Your life is meant to be lived at this specific time in our world's history. Sound kinda dramatic? It is! Your life ordained by our Creator is dramatic as it gets! You are His most valuable creation.

However, my heart aches when I look around this world and see so many people denying their Creator, searching for their identity outside of Him. So many are unaware of their life's immeasurable value.

I watched a video recently of a woman discussing her opinions on a variety of subjects. When asked whether she believes her and her children were created by God, she very adamantly denied that any of them were.

I thought that was so remarkably sad. Not only for her, but for her children to hear from their mother that God has nothing to do with them. This leaves them susceptible to an unending search for identity and purpose throughout their lives.

Similarly, sometimes the circumstances of one's birth can make them feel God has not been present in their life. We all know pregnancies don't always come about through ideal circumstances. Some pregnancies are unplanned. Some are even a result of tragic events. Many children who are products of tragic circumstances have struggled with the knowledge of how they came to be, carrying the weight of this knowledge into adulthood. How does God play a role in their existence? God certainly did not want any woman to be abused; therefore, many who are conceived from abusive circumstances are perplexed to think how God would have anything to do with their existence.

Their thoughts can easily turn to thoughts of worthlessness; that they are an accident, merely a product of sperm and egg.

The IVF process and Jason's encounter shows, however, that there is separation from the start of the biological process (conception) to the time God chooses to ordain a life (embryo attachment). I believe this is why IVF was such an important part of our story. The IVF process is specific and time sensitive. It allows you to know when each step of the fertility process is taking place. Sperm and egg are placed together; you wait to see if an embryo is formed; then you have an embryo transfer into the uterus. Once transferred, you wait twelve to thirty-six hours to see if the embryo will attach to the uterine wall.

Attachment to the uterine wall is what determines a viable pregnancy. Without attachment to the mother, life will not exist. Without attachment, pregnancy hormones will not be detected days later to procure a positive pregnancy test. During this twelve to thirty-six hour wait to see if our embryos would attach, Jason encountered the angels in our room, who communicated to him this is how it happens every time God creates life.

I believe this separation from the time of conception to the time the embryo attaches to the uterine wall may give a new perspective to many. If you are one who seemingly came about from tragic circumstances, the urgency I felt to share our experience is for you to know your life is no accident. God did not ordain any tragedy associated with your conception, but sometime during the twelve to thirty-six hours pending attachment, God did indeed ordain you! Your value is not determined by the circumstances of your conception; your value is determined by your Creator, Who, despite your circumstances, saw an opportunity to place an eternal soul in an earthly vessel. He did for you what He does for all of us. He takes the circumstances the enemy means for evil and turns them into something beautiful!

This knowledge of God as Creator is what makes all the difference in any person's life. Without understanding our life's connection to the Creator at the very beginning of our existence, we the created will never truly be fulfilled. We will always be aimlessly searching to try to fill a void in our lives that can never be filled by anything or anyone else. Nothing and no one can validate our worth—not our occupation, our wealth, our spouse, or our friends. Our worth is validated by our Creator.

With that being said, for those who may have never been told, and for all who could use this beautiful reminder:

Your value is not determined
by the circumstances of
your conception; your
value is determined by
your Creator, Who, despite
your circumstances,
saw an opportunity to
place an eternal soul
in an earthly vessel.

God created your inmost being; you were knit together in your mother's womb. You are fearfully and wonderfully made! God's works are wonderful! Your frame was not hidden from Him when you were made in the secret place, when you were woven together in the depths of the earth. God's eyes saw your unformed body; all the days ordained for you were written in His book before one of them came to be (Psalm 139:13–16).

Even the very hairs on your head are number-ed, because you are so valuable to Him! (Matthew 10:30–31).

God knows the plans He has for you; He declared it! They are plans to prosper you, and not to harm you. Plans to give you hope and a future! (Jeremiah 29:11).

He loves you with an everlasting love and will continue His faithfulness to you! (Jeremiah 31:3).

For God so loved you, that He sent His one and only Son for you, to give you everlasting life! (John 3:16).

So cast every one of your cares upon Him, because He cares for you! (1 Peter 5:7).

And know that you are more than a conqueror through Him who loves you! Neither death nor life, neither angels nor demons, neither the present nor the future, nor any powers, neither height nor depth, nor anything else in all creation, will be able to separate you from the love of God in Christ Jesus! (Romans 8:37–39).

For though the mountains be shaken and the hills be removed, His unfailing love for you will Not be shaken or His promise of peace removed (Isaiah 54:10).

Chapter 10

A HEALING BALM

E'VE TOLD OUR STORY TIME AND TIME AGAIN, but I have no doubt we will continue to analyze and contemplate what we have experienced for years to come. I'm sure it will be studied by many reading as well. We want it to be reviewed. We love to hear interpretations of our story. We want people to think about what this story means to them, how it makes them feel. Does it validate or change their previous perception of God, angels, and supernatural experiences?

I've enjoyed researching angel encounters throughout Scripture as well as stories I've heard from others who have had angel encounters to see if I could find similarities or differences regarding our experiences.

Angels are creations of God. Genesis 2:1 says, "Thus the heavens and the earth, and all of the hosts of them, were finished." This informs us that angels were created before man. Most would agree angels are mentioned or referenced around three hundred times throughout Scripture.

Throughout history and even in present-day encounters, angels have had differing roles. The encounters that I will reference in this book barely scratch the surface of all the fascinating ways angels have been used by God.

Sometimes angels are "ministering angels" and "guardian angels" who care for or guard a specific person or group of people. Matthew 4 tells the story of Jesus's temptation. He was hungry after forty days of fasting, and Scripture gives the beautiful depiction of angels coming to his assistance:

> Now when the tempter came to Him, he said, "If You are the Son of God, command that these stones become bread."

But He answered and said, "It is written, 'Man shall not live by bread alone, but by every word that proceeds from the mouth of God.'" (vv. 3–4)

After continuous attempts by the enemy, verse 11 states:

Then the devil left Him, and behold, angels came and ministered to Him.

Other angels are "supernatural rescuers." We see this supernatural rescuing ability played out in Acts 12. During Herod's reign of violence over the church, James was killed and Peter arrested. An angel attended to Peter's needs and assisted in freeing Peter from jail:

Peter was therefore kept in prison, but constant prayer was offered to God for him by the church.

And when Herod was about to bring him out, that night Peter was sleeping, bound with two chains between two soldiers; and the guards before the door were keeping the prison.

Now behold, an angel of the Lord stood by him, and a light shone in the prison; and he struck Peter on the side and raised him up, saying, "Arise quickly!" And his chains fell off his hands.

Then the angel said to him, "Gird yourself and tie on your sandals"; and so he did. And he said to him, "Put on your garment and follow me."

So he went out and followed him, and did not know that what was done by the angel was real, but thought he was seeing a vision.

When they were past the first and second guard posts, they came to the iron gate that leads to the city, which opened to them of its own accord; and they went out and went down one street, and immediately the angel departed from him.

And when Peter had come to himself, he said, "Now I know for certain that the Lord has sent His angel, and has delivered me from the hand of Herod and from all the expectation of the Jewish people." (vv. 5–11)

We find another great example in Exodus 14, which tells how an angel accompanied Israel from Egypt to the promised land as they crossed the Red Sea on dry ground:

And the Angel of God, who went before the camp of Israel, moved and went behind them; and the pillar of cloud went from before them and stood behind them.

So it came between the camp of the Egyptians and the camp of Israel. Thus it was a cloud and darkness to the one, and it gave light by night to the other, so that the one did not come near the other all that night.

Then Moses stretched out his hand over the sea; and the LORD caused the sea to go back by a strong east wind all that night, and made the sea into dry land, and the waters were divided.

So the children of Israel went into the midst of the sea on the dry ground, and the waters were a wall to them on their right hand and on their left. (vv. 19–22)

The Reverend Billy Graham stated in his book *Angels: God's Secret Agents*, "I am convinced that these heavenly beings exist and that they provide unseen aid on our behalf." He shared a story I absolutely love in chapter 1 of this same book that exemplifies the supernatural way angels have been known to come to our aid in time of need:

❧

The Reverend Billy Graham stated in his book *Angels: God's Secret Agents*, "I am convinced that these heavenly beings exist and that they provide unseen aid on our behalf."

❧

The Reverend John G. Paton, a missionary in the New Hebrides Islands, tells a thrilling story involving the protective care of angels. Hostile natives surrounded his mission headquarters one night, intent on burning the Patons out and killing them. John Paton and his wife prayed all during that terror-filled night that God would deliver them. When daylight came they were amazed to see the attackers unaccountably leave. They thanked God for delivering them.

A year later, the chief of the tribe was converted to Jesus Christ, and Mr. Paton, remembering what had happened, asked the chief what had kept him and his men from burning down the house and killing them. The chief replied in surprise, "Who were all those men you had with you there?" The missionary answered, "There were no men there; just my wife and I." The chief argued that they had seen many men standing guard—hundreds of big men in shining garments with drawn swords in their hands. They seemed to circle the mission station so that the natives were afraid to attack. Only then did Mr. Paton realize that God had sent His angels to protect them. The chief agreed that there was no other explanation.[*]

These accounts are tangible examples confirming the truth of the following verses that have always been dear to my heart. Psalm 34:7 says, "The angel of the Lord encamps around those who fear Him, and delivers them." Similarly, Psalm 91:11 says, "For He shall give His angels charge over you, to keep you in all your ways."

Angels are also messengers sent to announce or communicate an important piece of information. Of course, the angel Gabriel's announcement to Mary of the coming birth of Christ in Luke 2 is one of the most well-known angel announcements. Later, when Christ was born, an angel brought "good tidings of great joy" to a group of shepherds, telling them where the newborn Christ could be found:

And suddenly there was with the angel a multitude of the heavenly host praising God and saying:

"Glory to God in the highest,

---

[*] Billy Graham, *Angels: God's Secret Agents* (Nashville, TN: Thomas Nelson, 2000)

And on earth peace, goodwill
toward men!" (Luke 2:14)

Another truth I love, shared by Reverend Billy Graham in the aforementioned book, is this: "Of one thing we can be sure: angels never draw attention to themselves but ascribe glory to God and press His message upon the hearers as a delivering and sustaining word of the highest order."

This was the case for Jason that night in our room. The angels were very direct with him concerning the message they were delivering—that what Jason witnessed that night is how we all come into existence by our Creator's hands. Although this book is entitled *Angels in Our Room* and although it was an amazing experience to have encountered these heavenly beings, we are quick to point out we are not wanting to glorify the angels. Rather, we want to proclaim the truth of the message the angels brought to us that night and glorify the Creator, whose message they were assigned to deliver.

Angels are also mentioned all throughout Revelation, which we know to be the book of future prophecy. Revelation 1:1 states, "The Revelation of Jesus Christ, which God gave Him to show His servants—things which must shortly take place."

Written by John, Revelation can seem confusing, even scary, as so much of the book is written using descriptions of frightening images and mysterious symbolic meanings. However, the book of Revelation is actually a book of hope and encouragement, with its central message being this: in the end, God is the Victor, winning the final battle over evil.

My uncle and aunt shared with us the significance of there being *three* angels in our room. When we contemplate angels having the role of messengers, why couldn't just one angel have come into our room and given us the message we needed to hear? Why three? They brought to our attention that our story reminded them of the three angels in Revelation. The first angel declared God as the One true Creator and this message to worship God as Creator should be shared to the whole world (Revelation 14:6). This is the core of our story's message. Jason saw an incredible glimpse of the process in which God creates life. When Jason realized he was viewing the process by which God was creating her, literally forming our daughter in my womb, he fell to the side of the bed in involuntary worship of the very Creator that the first angel of Revelation proclaimed.

The second angel declared, "Babylon is fallen" (v. 8) and then later instructed the people to "Come out

When Jason realized he was
viewing the process by which
God was creating her, literally
forming our daughter in my
womb, he fell to the side
of the bed in involuntary
worship of the very Creator
that the first angel of
Revelation proclaimed.

of [Babylon]" (18:4). What is Babylon? The English words *Babel* and *Babylon* are derived from the Hebrew word meaning "confusion." So the second angel was saying, "Come out of confusion." I see confusion everywhere in our society. When we attribute our lives to being merely a biological process and deny the fact there is a Creator of that process, we will forever be searching for ways to overcome our feelings of inadequacy. This causes confusion. We the creation cannot fully understand our identity until we understand our identity is found in the Creator. When our identity is not grounded in the truth that we are created by Him, we are susceptible to believe a multitude of lies—lies of the enemy of our soul, lies of our society that boast if you're not happy with who you are, then you can change you're very identity. This type of thinking— that God's creation can be changed to what man wills it to be—will be the downfall of any person or society, bringing nothing but pain and disappointment. If one denies his Creator, he is actually denying himself from the experience of receiving true fulfillment in the purpose God originally intended for his life. One's identity, fulfillment, and purpose is found connected to the Creator.

The third angel's message can seem frightening with its references to the end times message of the mark of the beast and wrath of God (14:9). However, I'm reminded that Jason, too, was scared when he was awakened in the middle of the night. However, when realizing there were angels in our room, he was filled with a peace like he'd never felt before. We can apply this same concept to the meaning of the third angel's message, which is this: "Look, there is an enemy of our soul. If we follow his ways and forsake God our Creator, it brings nothing but heartache, confusion, and death; and with that, fear. When we remember our Creator and His laws, we win! We win in life, and even unto death; in this we find peace."

The three angels' messages in Revelation are such an interesting interpretation of our story. We had never thought of it this way until it was brought to our attention. It's exciting, and we believe this is one of many interpretations! I've been amazed how God uses this story. We tell it the same way every time, yet it speaks to people in ways that are unique to them personally.

Jason and I had an opportunity to share our story with Geron Davis, one of our favorite songwriters. He said it reminded him of a study a good friend of his had once shared with him. His friend is a pastor and studied the origins and meanings of certain scriptures.

This pastor said that the verse "Thou anointest my head with oil" (Psalm 23:5, KJV) is often quoted in present-day sermons. The image that sometimes comes to mind is of Old Testament priests holding a horn filled with oil, from which the priest would administer oil for anointing. However, the pastor said the verse actually refers to shepherd practices of that day.

When shepherds would take care of their flock, they would use oil on the sheep's head, covering the sheep's eyes and ears, to keeps bugs and pestilence out. They also wanted the scent of the shepherd to be on the sheep, as the wolves weren't afraid of the sheep, but they were afraid of the shepherd. When wolves would attack, they would attack the sheep in the back of their heads, thus another reason the shepherd wanted their scent on the head of the sheep. The pastor used this as an analogy for current society. So many times, when the enemy of our soul attacks, he starts by attacking our minds and our thoughts with his lies.

Like the analogy of the shepherds anointing their sheep's heads, Geron shared with us that he felt God would use our story as a "healing balm" to many; some walking through the heartache of infertility, some needing a miracle, and some needing to hear the truth that their life was created and valued by God. But he also thought it would be used in ways maybe not yet revealed, because the story has many layers and will speak to and touch hearts in a very specific way, personal to each individual's situation.

We were so encouraged by his assessment, because even before he shared his feelings about our story, our prayer for those hearing our story was extraordinarily similar to how he felt God would use it. A healing balm! I couldn't love or agree with his description more. It has become my prayer for this book: "Lord, let Your love, power, and truth be revealed through our story. Let it be a healing balm to all who read it."

As I bring this book to its conclusion, I give God all the glory for everything He has done in our lives. He has been so good to us, despite ourselves. Jason and I are two very ordinary people with a multitude of shortcomings and failures. God didn't perform these miracles because we were perfect in any way. Just the opposite. We were broken. We acknowledged we needed the Great Physician if we were to have any hope of a child. He filled us with hope during every phase of our infertility journey and answered beyond our expectations.

❧

God didn't perform these
miracles because we were
perfect in any way. Just the
opposite. We were broken. We
acknowledged we needed the
Great Physician if we were
to have any hope of a child.

❧

With the knowledge God revealed in our story, many of us can be filled with hope. Those longing for a child are filled with hope to know God is the Giver of life, so an infertility diagnosis is not the end of your dreams to have a child. God will answer in one way or another, and whatever way that is, you can rest assured it is the best answer for you. Expect an answer that exceeds your expectations!

Believers are filled with hope. Hope to know God is still in the miracle-working business. He listens; He cares; He guides us along this journey we call life. Sometimes he leads with His sweet Holy Spirit and sometimes through a supernatural encounter. He is ever interceding on our behalf.

Those whose life came to be by what may seem to some an unconventional way, even a tragic way, are also filled with hope! The circumstances of your conception do not define you; your Creator does!

There is hope for every one of us. The magnificent process of creation is intentional and specific, showing God's handiwork in our lives from the very beginning. Each one of us are here on this earth because God willed us to be. Any life that ever was or will be is wanted, loved, and valued by the Creator. We all have a purpose, and with this comes hope!

Hope to know we are not alone on this journey we call life. He does not leave us to navigate life's ups and downs. He longs to guide us and fulfill His purpose throughout our lives.

If all this wasn't enough, we also have the hope of heaven. Jason and I have thought about heaven in a way we never did before this experience. We've always believed in heaven, but it's so much sweeter now. I think it's because it's no longer just a place we've heard of. We've had an actual encounter with angels who were sent down from this place—from another realm, another world, so to speak.

It has put our humanness into perspective. It has put this world and how fleeting it is into perspective. God has a purpose for every life on this planet, but another world, our heavenly home, awaits. Heaven is not ravished with pain and confusion. It is without sickness, affliction, or death. It's a place of perfect peace and rest created for us—His most valued creation. This knowledge brings us hope! This hope for every one of us is found in connection with our Creator and salvation through His Son, Jesus Christ. Nothing else in this life will bring us true joy or peace of mind.

I leave you with a favorite blessing of mine that my pastor uses at the end of every church service at our home congregation. He paraphrases Numbers 6:24-26 and combines those verses with a variety of phrases from the Psalms. This is my prayer over every single one of you.

≈

May the Lord bless and keep you;
May He make His face shine on
you and be gracious to you;
May He turn His countenance
toward you and grant you peace.
In your rising up, in your laying
down, in your going out, and coming
in, both now and forevermore.

ACKNOWLEDGMENTS

To God be all the glory!
Great things He has done!

O MY INCREDIBLE HUSBAND, JASON: THANK YOU so much for your never-ending love and support as I have endeavored to share our story. As in life, you have been by my side throughout every step of this process, cheering me on and affirming your love. I love you and I'm grateful we get to walk this road of life together.

Thank you to every one of my cherished family members and amazing friends who have prayed over this book and encouraged me to share it. You'll never know how much your support has meant to me. Every listening ear, every prayer uplifted, every word of advice and extension of love has not gone unnoticed. I love you all so much.

A special thanks to the incomparable team at Forefront Books and Simon and Schuster. What a fantastic experience it has been to work with each one of you.

Thank you to Ed Leonard; my brother, Rick Shelton; Dusty Wells; and the entire team at Daywind Music Group for producing the remarkable single "Angels in the Room" to accompany this book. My precious brother, what a joy it has been to work with you; thanks for championing this project. Geron Davis, your anointed writing is a gift to us all; what an honor it was to write this song with you. Amy Perry, your outstanding voice took this song to the next level. Thank you all from the bottom of my heart.

Thank you to my uncle Danny Shelton and Three Angels Broadcasting Network for providing your exceptional facilities to record the audio version of this book. You and Aunt Yvonne continually play an integral role in sharing our story, and I thank you and love you both dearly.

Carolyn Cross, you have poured your heart into our family in too many ways to count. We are forever grateful for your guidance and contributions of love from the very beginning of this book. Your musical composition for the audio version of this book is so beautiful and full of inspiration. We love you and thank you.

Tyler and Tiara, I am so proud to be your auntie. God brought both of you to our family in such special ways. I thought of you two often while writing. God has special plans for each of you and I can't wait to watch it all unfold. You have my heart and my love, always.

To contact GL Mendehall and to download the song "Angels in the Room" written by Geron Davis and GL Mendenhall, scan the QR Code.